COLLINS POCKET REFERENCE

SCOTTISH COUNTRY DANCING

Compiled in association with
The Royal Scottish Country Dance Society

Edited by Peter Knight

HarperCollins*Publishers*

HarperCollins Publishers
PO Box, Glasgow G4 0NB

First published 1996

Reprint 10 9 8 7 6 5 4 3

ISBN 0 00 470987 X

A catalogue record for this book is available from the British Library

Distributed in the United States by
Roberts Rinehart Publishers
6309 Monarch Park Place
Niwot
Colorado 80503

Printed and bound in Great Britain by
Caledonian International Book Manufacturing, Glasgow

Contents

Foreword

As President of The Royal Scottish Country Dance Society, I am delighted to have been given an opportunity to contribute to this publication. This book will, I am sure, prove to be a valuable addition to the library of many dancers, providing an introduction into most forms of Scottish dancing.

There are of course many different ways in which people have been introduced to this wonderful pastime, combining as it does the traditions of dancing in its earliest known forms with recently devised dances.

Most forms of dancing are embraced within the book, which includes the traditional dances as recorded and promoted by The Royal Scottish Country Dance Society, as well as the party dances commonly practised at balls, weddings and dances in Scotland, and indeed in many other countries.

Scottish country dancing has been inspired by the traditional music of the fiddle, bagpipe, and piano, and more recently the accordion. The reel, jig and strathspey are the principal rhythms, although some dances are in waltz or march tempo.

To all those who wish to enjoy the pleasures of social dancing combined with the appreciation of music, this book should prove invaluable.

The Earl of Mansfield
Scone Palace

Introduction

So you have been invited to a Scottish/Highland ball, wedding or ceilidh, you have found out the 'where', the 'when', the 'with whom', maybe the 'what to wear' and all you need is the 'know-how' to join in the dance!

The following chapters will explain the steps, formations and music for the popular dances you will want to learn. It is helpful to get together with members of your party to practise, but remember much of the sociability of dancing comes from meeting new friends as you dance round the room or progress down a set. It is considered impolite to form sets on the floor before a dance has been announced – however keen you are! When you join a longwise set, it must always be at the bottom. Never join in the middle, just because you want to dance with your friends.

As you take to the dance floor you may notice that all is not exactly as described in this book. Dancing is a living tradition and has evolved from many sources. Variations, therefore, occur which are dependent on area, social standing, and type of function. One difference you may notice is that some dancers, both male and female, are wearing soft-soled shoes while others are wearing everyday shoes – anything from brogues to trainers! This is a personal preference and makes no difference to the enjoyment of the dance, nor is it any indication of proficiency!

There are normally four couples in a longwise set. However, at some events, you will find sets counted in fives and, occasionally, in sixes. The Master of Ceremonies liaises with the band about the music and he will announce to the company how the sets are to be counted. Try not to insist on doing it your way even if that is the only way you have practised. Make sure that each couple has the opportunity to dance as top couple and enjoy the dance no matter how many times through it is played.

You need to be aware that floors can be slippery and sometimes the music is fast. On such occasions, it is necessary to adapt your dancing to the conditions and avoid accidents and injuries – no uncontrolled birls!

Some of the steps are not always performed as described in this book. Sometimes a circle in reel or jig time will be danced using slip step and sometimes with a gentle, lilting walking step. Some think the former is correct, others would never think of doing anything but the latter and some will quite happily join in either way. The most important thing is to be in time with the music.

Scottish music is wonderfully exhilarating, dancing to it is always a pleasurable experience – enjoy the dance!

Acknowledgements

My sincere thanks are due to all the devisors and collectors of dances for their generosity in allowing their dances to be published and for permitting the RSCDS to receive their royalties.

My gratitude also goes to members of the Publications and Research Committee of the RSCDS and other friends who have given help and support during the production of this book; I would especially like to thank Roz Scott Huxley for reproducing various sections of the RSCDS publication, *Manual of Scottish Country Dancing*, Alastair MacFadyen and Muriel Johnstone for re-writing their material on the Society and on music, Alan MacPherson for co-ordinating the drawings, Irene Bennett for the introduction, Linda Gaul for the *Hints on Reeling*, and the Earl of Mansfield for contributing the foreword.

The British Council of Ballroom Dancing have kindly given permission for the following dances for which they hold the copyright to be published in the collector's form: 'Boston Two Step', 'Highland Schottische', 'Military Two Step' and 'Veleta'. I apologise in advance to any copyright holders whose dances may appear in this book and who have not been credited; considerable effort has been expended on ensuring that copyrights have been traced and acknowledged but if there are any errors of either omission or commission, then I would welcome correspondence on this matter so that it can be corrected in later printing.

I hope that readers will benefit from this book and that they will enjoy their dancing all the more as a result.

Peter Knight

Dances most commonly found in the programs of Highland balls and reeling parties

All these dances are recorded on one CD: 'Music for Collins Pocket Reference Scottish Country Dancing (Vol. Two)' [RSCDS - CD9]

Dances suitable for beginners, children and parties

Auld Lang Syne

Verse 1
Should auld acquaintance be forgot
    And never brought to mind?
Should auld acquaintance be forgot
    And auld lang syne!

Chorus
For auld lang syne, my dear,
    For auld lang syne
We'll tak a cup o' kindness yet
    For auld lang syne.

Verse 2
And there's a hand my trusty fiere!
    And gie's a hand o' thine!
And we'll tak a right gude-willie waught
    For auld lang syne.

Chorus

INSTRUCTIONS

Verse 1 & 1st chorus Company stands in a large circle with nearer hands joined, arms gently swinging.

Verse 2 Each person crosses own arms and re-joins hands, right in left with person on either side and arms are gently moved up and down.

2nd chorus With arms still crossed, company advances and retires (twice), with the music speeding up.

The Scottish Country Dance

AN HISTORICAL SKETCH

When the Scottish Country Dance Society was formed in Glasgow on 26th November 1923, its first stated aim was to practise and preserve country dances as danced in Scotland. What were the country dances, what were their origins and how had they developed as a form of social dance?

The country dance has a number of characteristics. It is a form of social dancing danced by a group of couples, nowadays usually consisting of four couples, positioned adjacent to each other in two parallel lines, the gentlemen facing the ladies.

An important feature of the longwise country dance is that it is progressive. At the conclusion of each turn of the dance, the couple at the top, who begin the dance, finish one place further down the set, eventually arriving at the bottom of the set. Then each of the other couples in succession, having reached the top, take their turn of the dance in order to progress to the bottom.

The country dance was, and still is, danced progressively mostly in longwise sets. There are, however, other dances which have been incorporated into the repertoire of country dancers. For example, there are those which have a square set formation, and others which have two-couple sets and require the dancers to move progressively round the ballroom.

The country dance is composed of formations which are arranged in a different sequence for each dance. Having mastered the basic formations, it has always been contended that a country dancer should be able to participate happily and easily wherever there is country dancing.

Today, as in the past, the social character of the country dance is strongly emphasised. It is a form of dancing which enables the dancer to dance with and to meet many other dancers during

9

the course of an evening's dancing:

> ...in them [country dances] all are alike partakers of the plea-
> sure, – there are no silent, envious gazers, – no sullen critics to
> mar the amusement, or intimidate its votaries, – joyous gaiety
> animates every countenance, and, while pleasure beams in
> every eye, the young and old are equally employed in forming
> the mazy circlets of the dance.
>
> Robert and Joseph Lowe, teachers of dancing, Glasgow, 1822

Although they have been the subject of much scholarly specu-
lation, there is still uncertainty about the origins of the country
dance. In Scotland the country dance probably began to be
danced in the early years of the eighteenth century. This form of
social dance had already been popular in England for more than
a hundred years; the first important collection of country dances
was published there by John Playford in 1651. In fact, the country dance acquired enthusiastic adherents in several European
countries and during the eighteenth century its universal popularity increased greatly.

Evidence of this popularity can still be found and seen today.
There are, in several British towns and cities, eighteenth-century
assembly rooms which were constructed to accommodate the
sets of the country dance. In Edinburgh, the first public assembly
at which the country dances were performed was begun in 1723
and other Scottish towns and cities, Aberdeen, Glasgow, Inverness, Dundee, Leith and Haddington, had all acquired their
assemblies by the 1780s.

Further evidence of the country dance's popularity 200 years
ago is provided by the many published collections of country
dances. These publications, many of which have been gathered
together in libraries and archives, contained the directions for
the dances and the music to accompany them. The collections
were mostly printed and published in England. The first such

Scottish collection, which has survived, was that of John Bowie, published in Perth in 1789. There are in addition, several Scottish manuscript collections which further testify to the popularity of the country dance in eighteenth-century Scotland. An example of these is the Duke of Perth MS, dated 1737 and written by the Edinburgh writing master, David Young; it is to be found at Drummond Castle, Muthill, Perthshire. Another example is the Castle Menzies MS, dated 1749 and located in the Atholl Collection of the Sandeman Library, Perth.

Although essentially part of an international repertoire of country dancing, the country dances danced in Scotland during the eighteenth century did begin to develop their own distinctive Scottish characteristics. There were dances, for example, which were described as 'Scotch dances'. They were principally identified by their accompanying tunes which had Scottish titles and which invariably gave their names to the country dances. Examples of such dances are 'Cadgers in the Canongate', 'Cauld Kail in Aberdeen', 'The Duchess of Atholl's Slipper', 'The Moudiewort', and 'Monymusk'. Detailed studies of the historical development of the country dance in Scotland and elsewhere have also revealed that the formations 'set and turn corners followed by reels of three' were probably a Scottish contribution to the formations of the country dance.

In eighteenth-century Scotland another type of dancing, namely the reels, featured the reels of three and also reels of four. In the reels, three or four dancers alternated the dancing of the reel or figure of eight with individual setting steps. The attachment of the Scots to their reels was never diminished by the popularity of the country dances.

The general dance here [Edinburgh] is the reel which requires that particular sort of steps to dance properly of which none but the people of the country have any idea. The perseverance which the Scotch ladies discover in these reels is not the less surprising than their attachment to them in preference to all others… the moment one of these tunes is played, which is liquid laudanum to my spirits, up they start, animated with new life, and you would imagine they had been bit by a tarantula… The young people of England only consider dancing an agreeable means of bringing them together. But the Scotch admire the reel for its own merit alone, and may truly be said to dance for the sake of dancing.

Captain Edward Topham, a visitor to Edinburgh, 1774–5

Those who attended the grand and elegant assemblies of Scotland's towns and cities were, of course, the prosperous members of eighteenth-century society. It is, however, evident that the country dances as well as the reels were enjoyed by the lower classes of society particularly in the countryside where the gathering places for dancing were much less imposing than the Assembly Rooms of either Edinburgh or Glasgow. Robert Burns, the son of a struggling Ayrshire farmer, attended a dancing school in his youth.

Probably Scotland's most notable contribution to the tradition of country dancing is the strathspey rhythm which emerged in Scotland about the middle of the eighteenth century. With its characteristic 'dotted' rhythm, the strathspey was uniquely Scottish. An eminent composer and exponent of the strathspey, as well as of reels and jigs, was Niel Gow (1727–1807). His compositions for the fiddle, the principal and most favoured instrument to accompany the country dances, paid tribute in their titles to the well known and leading personalities of Scottish society.

The years immediately following the conclusion of the Napoleonic Wars in 1815 witnessed the spread of two new forms of dance in Europe, the waltz and the quadrille. When faced with these competitors, the country dance displayed remarkable adaptability by absorbing elements from both of these new dance forms. Waltz country dance has survived to the present as an example of country dances in waltz tempo. The quadrille, with its country dance formations presented in a square set, was developed in France but quickly spread to other countries after 1815. An amalgamation of the square formation of the quadrille with elements of the country dance, and also of the reel, produced the universally known Eightsome Reel. Lord James Stewart Murray, 9th Duke of Atholl, who was President of the Royal Scottish Country Dance Society for many years, maintained that the Eightsome Reel was devised by a group of dancers gathered at Blair Castle in the early 1870s.

For most of the eighteenth and nineteenth centuries, it was considered that the leading exponents of all forms of dance were to be found in France. The influence which French dancers and teachers exerted upon social and theatrical dancing was as evident in Scotland as elsewhere. The effects of that influence have survived in Scottish country dancing to the present day. Poussette, pas de basque and allemande have found a permanent place in country dance terminology and the influence of the French ballet can be seen in the use of the balletic foot positions to define the structure of the steps of the country dancers. The balletic influences are also evident in other forms of Scottish dancing, namely Highland solo dancing and Ladies' Step dancing; the latter, which are solo dances mostly dating from the first half of the nineteenth century, have enjoyed a considerable revival of interest in recent years with the encouragement of the Royal Scottish Country Dance Society.

The French influence was not limited solely to dancing style and technique. The rules of ballroom etiquette, still observed by Scottish country dancers, can probably be directly linked to the example set by French dancers and teachers, especially those at

Court. The ballroom guides which appeared in print in Scotland in the nineteenth and early twentieth centuries invariably included some guidance for dancers about how they should conduct themselves in the ballroom.

The country dance declined in popularity in Europe as the nineteenth century progressed; other new social dances proved to be more popular. The exception to this decline was in Scotland where the country dance continued to flourish alongside the new dances. A number of reasons have been offered to explain this. A tradition of dancing in the Scottish regiments, which has persisted to the present day, helped to ensure the favoured position of the country dance, as also did the support which it received from the Scottish nobility and gentry. However, the country dance was not the exclusive monopoly of the privileged classes for it appealed to all sections of the population. Evenings of social dancing were occasions, especially in rural Scotland, when all levels of society came together to enjoy the pleasures of the country dance.

Credit for the continued popularity of the country dance must also be given to the professional teachers of dancing. Whilst not excluding the other fashionable dances of the time, they did not neglect the country dance. In their classes, the dance teachers, who were predominantly male, accompanied themselves on the fiddle and in the countryside where their teaching was done on an itinerant basis, they were affectionately known as the 'dancies'.

By the outbreak of the First World War an unbroken tradition of country dancing had lasted in Scotland for more than 200 years. Although by 1914 the number of very popular dances had in fact dwindled to a very few, they nevertheless appeared regularly on dance and ball programmes. The same dances were often repeated several times during an evening.

In the years immediately following the First World War, the Scottish country dance faced an uncertain future. Dances inspired by the syncopated rhythms of ragtime threatened to oust it entirely from the ballroom. It was due to the efforts of the Royal Scottish Country Dance Society that it survived this crisis and was eventually restored to national and international favour.

ITS TYPE AND FORM

A country dance is composed of a sequence of formations. Descriptions of these are given in the chapter on steps and formations (p.36–92). A dance is completed when its entire sequence of formations has been danced. Each formation is allocated a particular phrase of the music and the duration of a dance is determined by the number of formations contained in it. To be danced through once, most dances require 32 bars of music but some have fewer or more bars.

Scottish country dances fall mainly into three types: longwise, round-the-room, and square.

Longwise dances

Most Scottish country dances are progressive and are danced in longwise sets. In a set, normally made up of four couples, partners face each other across the set, the man having his left shoulder to the top of the set. The top of the set is nearer to the source of music.

THE LONGWISE SET

Women	Men
4	4
3	3
2	2
1	1

TOP
MUSIC

Sets should not be too narrow and when space permits partners should be about two and a half yards apart, with approximately a single arm's length between each couple. The width and length of sets, however, may be varied.

In the longwise set, each couple, beginning from the top place, have the opportunity to dance as the leading or dancing couple. Once the leading couple begin to dance, they dance continuously until they reach the bottom of the set where they stand until they are needed. As the dance continues, they then begin to progress towards the top until at the completion of the dance all dancers have returned to their original positions.

Progressing in two-couple dances

In dances requiring two couples the dancing couple progress one place at a time and finish in the fourth place having completed the dance three times. The 2nd couple, as the new top couple, begin the dance on the third turn of the dance, the 3rd couple on the fifth and the 4th couple on the seventh. It is usual to dance a two-couple dance eight times, which means that the 4th couple dance twice only to finish in third place.

(i) Starting position		(ii) Positions at the end of the first time through the dance	
4	4	4	4
3	3	3	3
2	2	1	(1)
1	1	2	2
	TOP		TOP

16

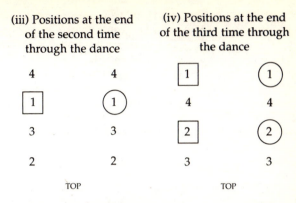

(iii) Positions at the end of the second time through the dance

4	4
1	(1)
3	3
2	2

TOP

(iv) Positions at the end of the third time through the dance

1	(1)
4	4
2	(2)
3	3

TOP

Progressing in three-couple dances

In dances requiring three couples, the top couple also progress one place at a time and finish in third place having completed the dance twice. The 2nd couple, as the new top couple, begin the dance on the third turn of the dance, the 3rd couple on the fifth, and the 4th couple on the seventh. A three-couple dance is

(i) Starting position

4	4
3	3
2	2
1	1

TOP

(ii) Positions at the end of the first time through the dance

4	4
3	3
1	(1)
2	2

TOP

(iii) Positions at the end of the second time through the dance	(iv) Positions at the end of the third time through the dance

4	4	1	1
[1]	(1)	4	4
3	3	[2]	(2)
2	2	3	3
TOP		TOP	

normally danced eight times, thus enabling each couple to dance twice. Having finished in the third place, it is usual for the dancing couple then to take the fourth place by moving behind the last couple, who step up one place. At the end of the eighth turn of the dance the dancing couple finish in third place.

Progressing in four-couple dances

In dances requiring four couples, each couple dance only once. Having started in the top place, the dancing couple normally finish in the fourth place (see figure opposite), although in some modern compositions, there are other variations. A four-couple dance is normally danced four times, a new top couple beginning on each repetition.

Square dances

In these dances, the dancers, positioned in a square formation, are numbered in a clockwise direction, beginning with the top couple, who are nearest the music (see figure opposite). Partners stand side by side, each woman on her partner's right. Although

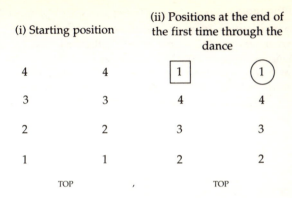

(i) Starting position		(ii) Positions at the end of the first time through the dance	
4	4	[1]	(1)
3	3	4	4
2	2	3	3
1	1	2	2
	TOP		TOP

Progressing in four-couple dances

THE SQUARE SET

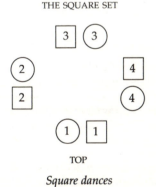

TOP

Square dances

circles are often a feature of the square dances, as, for example, in the Eightsome Reel, it is important that dancers are always aware that the essential shape of these dances is the square.

Round-the-room dances

In these dances the sets are arranged in one large circle round the room either with one couple facing another or with a line of three dancers facing another line of three as in Dashing White Sergeant. Dancers progress in the direction in which they originally faced. Partners pass the dancers with whom they have just danced to finish back to back with them. They are now ready to repeat the dance in a new set.

Sets for a two-couple round-the-room dance

THE GENERAL APPEARANCE OF THE DANCE

During an adjudication at a Scottish country dance festival, Miss Milligan exclaimed: 'It is a pity that there are so many performers and so few dancers'. The difference between 'performing' and 'dancing' has to be appreciated in order to bring out several important characteristics in Scottish country dancing.

Teamwork

Eight excellent performers, no matter how good their individual technique or their knowledge of the dance, can fail to make a really good team if they do not have a real sense of the value of teamwork.

Anticipation is important for good teamwork. Throughout each dance, whether dancing or waiting to join in, each dancer must observe all that is happening in the set and anticipate what is about to take place. In this way, the continuous flow of the dance is maintained.

The management of a set also contributes towards good teamwork. Some dances require greater or less width of set than others; some require, also, greater length than others. Not only should the dance start with the appropriate width and length to suit the movements of the dance and the capabilities of the dancers, but teamwork should help to maintain that size of set throughout each turn of the dance. In dances, such as 'The Triumph' or 'West's Hornpipe', where three couples all step up to let the dancing couple finish their turn in fourth place, special care must be taken to keep the whole set in the same position relative to other sets in the room. All dancers should be aware of, and helpful towards, other dancers outside their own sets. Special consideration has to be shown, too, where there is not much space between sets and where the dance involves casting or reels on the sidelines.

Another important feature of good teamwork is covering which requires an awareness by each dancer of his/her own position in relation to that of other dancers. In this way the pattern of the dance is clearly defined, especially in matching movements. Covering, together with correct phrasing, is the essence of good teamwork.

Phrasing

Good phrasing is the hallmark of the good dancer. Each formation has a definite phrase of music and dancers must begin the formation on the first beat of the phrase and complete the formation on the very last beat of the phrase.

Every step must be danced with the music and to achieve this, dancers must constantly be thinking ahead, judging the distance still to be travelled against the number of bars of music left in the phrase. This may mean that steps may have to be lengthened or shortened accordingly.

Good phrasing allows dancers to lead smoothly into the next formation, on the first beat of the next phrase, without any apparent break, yet knowing – and showing – that the previous formation has been completed within its own phrase but as part of the whole dance.

In dances where particular formations or movements are shown to take four, eight or even more bars of music, without detailed instructions on how the phrasing should be managed, it is the responsibility of each dancer to work out the correct phrasing, knowing the starting point, the finishing point and what has to be danced in between to the given number of steps. Too often dancers finish the formation or movement before the end of the musical phrase because they have not thought about the phrasing before they started and have not thought ahead during the dancing of the phrase.

Technique

Technique is not an end in itself but a means of maintaining one of the characteristics which sets Scottish country dancing apart from other forms of dance. Technique includes accurate footwork, use of hands, phrasing, covering and the use of the correct step or steps for specific movements.

As with all other skills, the learning and understanding of basic technique allows for the accomplishment of any activity to be achieved with ease and enjoyment. In Scottish country dancing, the enjoyment of any dance can only be enhanced by a thorough knowledge of basic technique.

Deportment

An upright carriage is essential for correct technique. Within physical limitations, each dancer should strive to achieve an easy, natural poise with no affectation. While dancing, the line of gravity should pass through the head to the supporting foot. There should be no excessive body movement.

Use of hands

The giving of hands is an essential characteristic of Scottish country dancing. They are given primarily as a help to other dancers, especially on a slippery floor. The shape of formations is emphasised by the correct positioning of hands and arms. In addition the giving of hands adds to the social aspect of the dance.

The general rule is that hands are given at shoulder height, with elbows down. There is no definitive rule about who gives hands to whom and how, but it is generally accepted that a man gives his hand to a woman, with the palm upwards. Where hands are joined in threes on the sidelines, before dancing advance and retire or six hands round and back, then the dancer in the middle of each line extends his or her hands, with palms upwards, to the dancers on either side. This middle dancer can then assist the dancers on either side to maintain the line during the advance and retire or to make and break the circle.

In setting to and turning corners in reel and jig time, two hands are always used with pas de basque steps; similarly, in strathspey time, two hands are used for turning corners after having set to them. In formations such as turning corner and partners, in grand chain, in rights and lefts, the 'shake hands hold' is used.

The term 'lead' now indicates that the right hands are joined, either for leading down the middle or for crossing or placing of the man's partner. By contrast, the term 'dance' indicates that nearer hands are joined. In earlier books published by the Society, the term 'lead' was generally used and could mean 'lead' or 'dance' as described above.

Bow and curtsey

This natural 'honouring' of one's partner should be simple and unaffected, be done rhythmically and lead on to the dance as the chord at the beginning of the music leads on to the playing of the melody.

If the chord is played

the bow and curtsey can be more easily fitted to the music: 'and, down – up'. Most bands, however, play the chord

but the same three movements have to be fitted to this music.

On the first note, the man draws himself up slightly; on the second, he bows from the waist, keeping his back straight and still looking at his partner; on the third, he returns to the starting position. Throughout, his arms are held naturally at his sides.

Similarly, on the first note, the woman draws herself up slightly; on the second, she places the toe of one foot close up to the heel of the other foot and bends both knees equally, keeping the body erect and looking at her partner; finally, she too returns to the starting position. It is a matter of individual preference which foot is placed behind.

While curtseying, and throughout the dance when she is moving, with her hands free, the woman may hold her full-length dress in order to lift it clear of her feet. It should be held towards the front, between the thumb and the first two fingers with the arms slightly curved. There is no need to hold a short dress.

Dance etiquette

Good manners should be the accompaniment of the Scottish country dance and should be evident even before the dance begins.

Couples wait until a dance is announced before making up sets. When they join others already on the floor, they should do so at the end of lines, without intruding on sets already made up. After the dance is finished, it is good manners to clear the floor.

In the dance itself, helpful, courteous use of hands, thoughtful stepping up or down, anticipation and awareness of other dancers, covering and phrasing are essential.

Spirit of the dance

Mastery of the skills which have been described may lead to the correct performance of the dance without, however, expressing the true spirit of the Scottish country dance – 'performing' rather than 'dancing'.

The expression of the true spirit cannot be taught; it comes from the stimulus of the music and each individual's response to the lively, elegant movements of the dance.

MUSIC

Scotland's rich heritage of music and dancing enjoys worldwide popularity. The collection and publication of old dances has safeguarded the correct performance of the dance and has led to enthusiastic research into Scottish dance music. A wealthy store of wonderful music exists in collections of old manuscripts and books gathered in libraries and archives.

Within Scottish traditional music there are many forms, but the three best known to the dancers of today are jig, reel, and strathspey. The repertoire also includes the hornpipe, lament, march pastoral, polka, rant, schottische, Scots Measure, slow air, concert strathspey, and song air. There is, today, much use of many of these forms of music for our country dances and, despite their own individual shape and characteristics, they have been considered suitable music for jig, reel, and strathspey dance forms. In particular, there has been a trend towards the use of slow airs for dancing strathspeys, and although these tunes are very popular with many dancers, there must be an awareness that they alter the strength and character of the strathspey step.

The one distinctive form that Scottish instrumental music can claim to have evolved is the Strathspey. The name and the musical form are practically all that remain to guide us in any inquiry into its historical beginnings. Conceived primarily as a musical accompaniment to the Scottish reel, the strathspey, as we have it, represents (like other art forms) an evolution, and no date can be assigned for its emergence. Published collections of strathspeys and reels did not appear till after the middle of the eighteenth century, by which time tunes like 'Tullochgorum' and 'The Reel of Tulloch' were already reckoned old. The strathspey and reel were originally bagpipe tunes and the pipe strathspey has remained pretty much fixed in form and scope, but when the fiddle composers took up the strathspey, the more extensive resources of the instrument encouraged and made possible a very considerable development in the form.

The first publication of fiddle music as such was a collection of *Scots Reels or Country Dances* published in Edinburgh by Robert Bremner (1757). There followed many collections from musicians all over the country; the collections of John Riddell of Ayr (1776) David Dow of Edinburgh (his collection of 1776 was the first to include the word 'strathspey' in its title); Joshua Campbell of

Glasgow (1779); Alexander McGlashan of Edinburgh (1780); Robert Petrie of Kirkmichael (1790); and Archibald Duff of Montrose (1794) are but a few. The greatest collections of this period came from the masters Niel Gow and his son Nathaniel, Robert Mackintosh, William Marshall, and Captain Simon Fraser. The aristocracy and landed gentry of this period subscribed to the collections and often the collections included not only dedications to these patrons but also compositions from the pen of these amateurs, such as Colonel Hugh Montgomery, Twelfth Earl of Eglintoun and Miss Lucy Johnston of Hilton.

Niel Gow, born in 1727 at Inver, near Dunkeld, was probably one of the first professional folk fiddlers of Scotland. Many of the other Scottish musicians of the time alternated between classical and folk music, earning their living from classical music. Niel enjoyed the patronage of three Dukes of Atholl during his long and lively life. He had a very distinguishable style of playing and a compositional output of over 80 tunes. He was in great demand to play at important balls and parties with his band.

Nathaniel Gow (born 1763) also earned his living from folk music, becoming the leader of the orchestra that played at fashionable events in Edinburgh. He started a publishing business and was also a fine composer – 'Largo's Fairy Dance' being probably one of the best known reels in the repertoire.

Robert Mackintosh (born 1745) dabbled in classical music but his heart was really in traditional Scottish music. He settled in Edinburgh and published four collections of music of a full, elegant style. 'Miss Campbell of Saddell' is a fine example.

Probably the most talented fiddle composer of the eighteenth century was William Marshall (1748–1833). His collection of 1822 is perhaps the finest single collection of Scottish fiddle music ever printed. In addition to dance music, Marshall wrote recital pieces entitled 'slow strathspeys', and Robert Burns gave him the accolade 'the first composer of strathspeys of the age'. His finest include 'The Marchioness of Huntly' and 'The Marquis of Huntly's Farewell'.

This was the end of one of the greatest periods of Scottish traditional music. High society turned to new fashions and dances, such as quadrilles, polkas, waltzes and mazurkas, but some of the gentry continued to patronise and support traditional music and the traditional country dances, especially in Perthshire. It was, however, in the north east of Scotland that traditional fiddle music regained its popularity in the late nineteenth century, mainly through the career of James Scott Skinner. He made his living as a teacher and dancing master around the north of Scotland. He toured extensively and included in his concert programmes both classical and traditional music. He is the only legendary fiddler of the past to have been recorded and some of these recordings have been re-issued. His output as a composer was vast, having over 600 pieces published; he was the last of the really great fiddle composers.

The interests and habits of society changed so much in the first half of the twentieth century that new dances, mainly from America, became the craze. More and more people enjoyed listening to radio, television and records resulting in less and less home entertainment. Despite a decline in interest in the early part of the century, fiddle music did survive, of course, through the efforts of several talented fiddlers, for example James F. Dickie of New Deer, the Hardie family of Methlick and 'Dancie' Reid of Newtyle; and the outlook has improved with the competitions, fiddle rallies and strathspey and reel societies attracting large numbers of players and enthusiastic audiences. Nor has composition come to a halt; many of the fiddlers, accordionists, pianists and pipers of the twentieth century have contributed fine music to the repertoire of Scottish dance music.

The accompaniment to the dance has altered over the centuries. Up until the early nineteenth century there were two

ypes of bagpipes in existence in Scotland - the Highland bagpipe and the Lowland or Border bagpipe. The Border pipes
became extinct largely because of the rise of the violin but bagpipe playing in the Highlands became more and more sophisti-
cated. The pipes are particularly associated with military activi-
ties and ceremonial occasions; at the other end of the range of
the pipe repertoire is classical solo pibroch and there is also a
tradition of piping for dancing – both Highland dancing and
country dancing.

Around the time of the Restoration (1660), the violin arrived in
Scotland and was to become one of Scotland's national instru-
ments. Craftsmen copied the famous Italian models, particularly
those of Amati and Guarnerius. Violin-making still flourishes in
Scotland today. Dancing the reels and country dances was a popular pastime in eighteenth-century Scotland and the violin was
ideally suited to accompany them.

During the era of the great fiddle composers, the fiddle was
the main instrument used to accompany the dance; often on its
own, sometimes with a 'cello to provide a bass line and steady
rhythm, or sometimes two fiddles played together. Then larger
groups were formed which could include, for example, recorder,
lute, oboe, bassoon, violins, 'cello, harpsichord and later, piano.
Many of the fiddle collections were published for violin or German
lute with bass, and these versions were often played on the piano.

In the twentieth century, the accordion came to be strongly
associated with Scottish dance music. A typical line-up in a present-day Scottish country dance band would include fiddle,
accordion(s), piano, bass and drums. The availability of recorded
and broadcast music of all sorts, together with the different
instrumentation has altered the interpretation of traditional
Scottish music since the days of the solo fiddler.

The music of Scotland is on the one hand strongly evocative,
and on the other, very conducive to lively, spirited dancing. The

importance of the part the music plays in the general appearance of the dance cannot be overstressed. Miss Jean Milligan (co-founder of The Royal Scottish Country Dance Society) said: 'The music is the stimulus of the dance and the dance should be the physical expression of the music'. To aid good dancing, the music must be well executed, rhythmically strong, well phrased, have light and shade and be played at a suitable tempo for the steps required. Scottish country dance music requires considerable practice to accomplish a standard of playing which produces the necessary rousing spirit for the dancers. Far too many people, however, do not listen to the music and therefore lose the stimulus and flow given by it. The dance should become an integral part of the music and the music an integral part of the dance; therefore, it is of vital importance that the dance musician has knowledge of the steps, formations and dances to be able to enter fully into the spirit of the movements and so make music that does give the correct impulse.

At the time of the founding of the Royal Scottish Country Dance Society there was a lack of elegance on the dance floor and only through sound teaching of technique, accompanied by good music, was Scottish country dancing restored to its former dignity. It would be foolish to be dictatorial on the subject of speed for dancing; any speed indications given should always be treated merely as a guide to setting the tempo. Often, it is more a matter of vitality in the music that provides the lift required for dancing rather than a rigid adherence to an optimum tempo. There should always be sufficient time for the dancers to move easily through the formations of the dance. It is a misconception that music played quickly is more spirited. In fact, music which is too fast can only lead to lack of control in the dancers, careless footwork, poor rhythm, and a loss of overall poise and ease. Music played too slowly, however, often leads to the spirit of both dance and music being lost. Many musicians provide superb music and are very aware of the dancers' requirements and so uphold the traditional Scottish spirit of our dancing and music.

The tunes which are published in the Scottish country dance books are either the original traditional tunes used for the old dances or ones which match the various formations within the dance. When learning a dance, familiarisation with the original tune for that dance helps in remembering the figures. The musicians then have the difficult task, when selecting tunes for a particular dance, of maintaining the character and phrasing of the original tune in their choice of alternative tunes; too often tunes are selected only by virtue of their popularity rather than for their compatible character.

A vast amount of recorded music is available for Scottish dancing to suit all tastes. There is nothing more exciting, however, than dancing to good live music and there is fortunately no lack of enthusiastic players of a very high standard. It is a worthy tribute to the traditions of Scotland that her music and dance are so appreciated by so many people around the world.

NOTES ON THE MUSIC
Reel time
Tempo: just over 1/2 minute for 32 bars.
Time signatures: ¢, 2/2, c, 4/4, 2/4   2 or 4 beats in the bar.
Good for teaching pas de basque – even beats

Jig time
Tempo: similar to reel time.
Time signatures: 6/8   2 beats in the bar.
Good for teaching slip step and skip change of step. Skipping rhythm.

Strathspey time
Tempo: approximately 1 minute for 32 bars.
Time signatures ¢, 2/2, c, 4/4   2 or 4 beats in the bar.
A characteristic of the music is dotted rhythms – ♩♫ and ♫♩. – particularly the second grouping known as the Scotch snap.

The Royal Scottish Country Dance Society

In the years immediately following the First World War there was a revival of interest in traditional dance and song in England. The English Folk Dance Society (EFDS), which had been founded in 1911 by Cecil Sharp, had published several books of English country dances. These books were enthusiastically taken up by the recently formed Girl Guide Association and the dances they contained were taught to Guides in Scotland as well as England. Mrs Ysobel Stewart of Fasnacloich, who was then Guide Commissioner for Argyll, decided that it would be more appropriate for Guides in Scotland to learn Scottish country dances. To make that possible, a book, similar to those available from the EFDS was required. Mrs Stewart, therefore, wrote out in a notebook the Scottish dances which she had danced all her life; she also included the music to accompany them. With a view to publication, she then approached Michael Diack of the Glasgow publishers, Patersons, who agreed to undertake the project provided the correctness of the dances was verified. He arranged a meeting with Miss Jean Milligan of Jordanhill College, Glasgow. As a lecturer in physical education, Miss Milligan had included the Scottish dances in her work with student teachers. The two ladies met in the autumn of 1923 and agreed to go ahead with the publication of a book of twelve Scottish country dances and also to the formation of a society to give support to the new publication.

The Scottish Country Dance Society was formed on 26th November 1923 at a meeting held in Glasgow and attended by 27 people. The title 'Royal' was conferred upon the Society in 1951. The partnership of Miss Milligan and Mrs Stewart provided the Society with a firm foundation on which to grow and develop and from its small beginnings it has now become a worldwide organisation with a membership in 1994 of 25,000.

Glasgow and Edinburgh were the first cities to form branches of the Society. Branches in other parts of Scotland followed and eventually they were established throughout the United Kingdom. The expansion of the Society beyond Britain after the Second World War resulted in the emergence of the first overseas Branches. In 1994 the total number of Branches was 163.

The co-founders and their associates aimed to revive Scottish country dancing and to restore it to the ballroom in a dignified and sociable manner. To achieve that goal, and to allow country dancers to enjoy the country dances wherever they might be, a measure of standardisation had to be adopted. However, there was never an intention to impose a rigid and inflexible uniformity. Slight variations in the interpretations of dances published by the Society have emerged in different parts of the country since 1923. Such variations are acceptable, provided that they remain only slight and do not prove to be an obstacle to the enjoyment of dancers who may be unfamiliar with them.

From its earliest days the Society sought to promote and to maintain the standards it set in a number of ways. First, instruction was, and continues to be, available in classes organised by branches of the Society and by groups affiliated to it; second, since 1924, teaching certificates have been awarded to members who successfully complete a training course; third, a summer school, first held in St Andrews in 1927, has played a very significant part in spreading the Society's message. It offers classes for all levels of ability and now, reflecting the international character of the Society, brings together dancers from all over the world.

Whilst attaching importance to good standards of dancing and teaching, the RSCDS has always been anxious to emphasise the social character of Scottish country dancing. Above all it should be enjoyable, offering plenty of opportunity for friendship and fun. The combination of a correctness of dancing technique with a lively and spirited response to the country dances and their music was described by Miss Milligan as 'controlled abandon'. She also asserted:

> ...dancing is a joyous thing and must never become so drilled and detailed as to lose the natural social spirit, which should be aroused in the dancers by the lively movements of these national dances and the stimulus of their Scottish music.

The RSCDS has regularly published books of country dances and music. Some of the traditional dances contained in the books were collected from people who remembered them and were able to describe them. Such oral sources were inevitably limited in their supply of dances and, therefore, for other dances the Society has had to rely upon old printed books and manuscript collections. Present-day Scottish country dancers must be very indebted to Mrs Stewart, Miss Milligan, and other interested Society members, who, over the years, have spent many hours searching out dances, interpreting their eighteenth- and nineteenth-century descriptions and adapting them to meet twentieth-century requirements.

Many hours of diligent research have also been devoted to finding appropriate tunes for the dances selected for publication. From 1923 to the present day, the RSCDS has been very fortunate in the musicians who have espoused its cause. They have generously donated their time, knowledge and skills and musicians and dancers all over the world should be grateful to them not only for what they have contributed to the RSCDS but also for what they have added by their efforts to the store of Scotland's traditional melodies.

One of the consequences of the success of the RSCDS and of the growing popularity of country dancing has been the composition of new dances. From these compositions have emerged new formations and new forms of progression. Although initially committed only to traditional dances, in more recent times the

Society has selected some of the modern dances for publication. Whilst the Society has been willing to encourage new ideas in the modern compositions it has chosen for inclusion in its books, it has also been anxious to ensure that these new dances retained the essential characteristics of the traditional country dance.

The achievements of the RSCDS since 1923 are quite remarkable considering that progress has been made without any assistance from public funds. It has relied entirely upon the support given by members in branches of the Society and in affiliated and other groups. A membership which is truly international and which transcends age, class and culture testifies to the pleasure and enjoyment which the Scottish country dance bestows on those who participate in it.

Further information regarding the work and publications of The Royal Scottish Country Dance Society may be obtained from:

> The Secretary
> The Royal Scottish Country Dance Society
> 12 Coates Crescent
> Edinburgh
> EH3 7AF
>
> Tel.: 0131 225 3854
> Fax: 0131 225 7783

Videos showing the Society's work are also available: *Video of the Manual* showing techniques, steps, formations and some dances such as 'The Glasgow Highlanders' and *Dances from Book 39* (The Duke & Duchess of Edinburgh, The New Virginia Reel & The Robertson Rant).

Steps and Formations

STEPS

There are two main categories of steps in Scottish country dancing:

1. Travelling Steps
   - (a) Reel and Jig   Skip change of step
   -                         Slip step
   -                         Running step
   - (b) Strathspey   Strathspey travelling step

2. Setting Steps
   - (a) Reel and Jig   Pas de basque
   - (b) Strathspey   Strathspey setting step or common Schottische
   -                         Highland Schottische

The steps require good muscular control and must be executed with precision. This entails careful study of the foot positions, correct placing of the feet at all times and constant practice to make certain that the footwork is obviously in the Scottish tradition.

There are four basic positions of the feet. To achieve these positions correctly, the leg must be turned out from the hip, allowing the knee to be well turned out and the foot to be at an angle of 45 degrees.

 First position: the heels are together. The weight of the body is evenly balanced on both feet.

Second position: the working foot is placed to the side with the heels in line.

Third position: the heel of the working foot, in front, touches the hollow of the instep of the supporting foot.

Fourth position: the working foot is fully extended straight forward from First position.

Fourth Intermediate position: a variation of Fourth position, the working foot, from Third position in front, is fully extended diagonally forward, between Second and Fourth positions.

When dancing, these positions vary slightly. For example in strathspey setting step the foot, well turned out, reaches to Second position with the heel in line with the heel of the supporting leg. In pas de basque, the heel of the front foot in Third position is just over the instep of the back foot.

All the attributes of good posture are essential if the steps are to be performed correctly. The dancer must have easy carriage, straight from the waist up, with no swaying of the body.

The steps are danced on the ball of the foot, the heels should never touch the floor and the toes should be pointed downwards.

All steps begin from First position.

Reel and Jig

Skip change of step

This step is used to travel.

One skip change of step takes one bar of music.

Skip: Hop on the left foot and, at the same time, fully extend the right leg forward.

Step: Reach forward with the right foot into Fourth position.

Close: Bring the left foot behind the right foot to form Third position

Step: Reach forward again with the right foot into Fourth position.

Rhythm: Hop, step, close, step (or similar variations).

The rhythm of jig time is particularly suitable for the practice of this step. The character of the step is light and lively and should give the feeling of flight and easy movement.

POINTS TO OBSERVE

1. The hop at the beginning must be very positive, although it cannot be too high or the remainder of the step will become distorted. The extended leg should be a firm line from hip to toe, the knee turned out, straight but not stiff, the toe pointed down and approximately two inches clear of the floor. This leading foot then reaches forward into Fourth position; it is not just placed down.

2. Each time the feet close in Third position, the instep of the rear foot makes contact with the heel of the front foot, but is not tucked under that heel. This should be automatic when the heels are not too high and when the feet are at the correct angle.
3. At the end of the step the back foot is brought through and the leg extended, ready to repeat the step.

Skip change of step is also used to travel backwards, as in Advance and Retire. Again, there must be a distinct hop to begin the step. The movement is 'hop, back, close, back' with the 'close' in this instance coming in front.

The foot travelling from the front through to the back, goes straight from Fourth position in front to Fourth position behind, the knee turned out, the toe towards the floor.

Pas de basque

This step is used for setting, for turning when two hands are given and sometimes for progressing over a limited distance.

One pas de basque step takes one bar of music. In Scottish country dancing 'to set' means one pas de basque step on the right foot and one on the left. It follows therefore that 'to set twice' means four pas de basque steps.

There are three distinct beats to each step. It is helpful to learn the step in the following stages:

1. With the right foot, step to the right into Second position and place the weight on the right foot. Bring the left foot to Third position in front of the right foot, with a transfer of weight onto the left foot and bring the right foot off the floor.

   Change the weight onto the right foot again and bring the left foot off the floor.

   Beginning with the left foot, the step is then repeated to the left.

2. When a positive change of weight has been established on beats two and three and the rhythm is automatic, begin the step with a spring into Second position, counting 'jump, beat, beat'.
3. To complete the foot positions of the step, the jeté is added. On the third beat, as the weight is transferred to the back foot the front foot is extended diagonally from Third position to Fourth Intermediate position, leg straight, toe pointed down, approximately two inches from the floor.

   From this Fourth Intermediate position, the step is then repeated beginning with the left foot, with the addition of 'and' to the count, to cover the transition.
4. Finally, the step must be danced on the spot, and not from side to side.

Rhythm: step, beat, beat and… spring, beat, beat and …

The rhythm of reel time is particularly suitable for the practice of this step, as it gives four even beats, whereas in jig time, the time between beats one and two, is fractionally longer than that between beats two and three.

POINTS TO OBSERVE

1. When danced on the balls of the feet and with the feet at the correct angle, the heel of the front foot in Third position will be just over the instep of the back foot. Care must be taken that, without raising the knee too high, the foot should come into this position from above and not from the side.
2. The jeté must never be omitted, as it is the distinctive element of the Scottish form of the pas de basque. Although it is a positive movement and should therefore be moderately emphasised, there is no need for an exaggerated extension.
3. Pas de basque, used as a travelling step, is for movements

where limited travel is required. It may be danced in any direction, as in set advancing, poussette or petronella. The distance to be travelled is usually comparatively short and must be completely covered on the first movement of the pas de basque. The step then continues as before, closing in Third position in *front* and followed by the jeté. The last beat of the bar is a moment of transition when the jeté moves on to the line of travel necessary for the following step. When travelling with pas de basque, it is particularly important to keep the angle of the feet correct and to close in Third position in front, in order to maintain the accuracy of the step.

Slip step

This step is used to travel sideways. It may be danced in circles with hands joined, or with dancers facing partners, both hands joined, to slip down or up or across the dance.
Two slip steps take one bar of music.
1. With left foot, step left into Second position.
2. Close right foot to left foot, heels touching, as in First position. When the heels touch, both feet are momentarily off the ground. This is repeated as often as is necessary.

Rhythm: 'step-together, step-together' is equal to one bar of music.

Slip step should be danced lightly, fairly high on the ball of the foot and with supple ankle movements. Body weight must be restrained, with no impression of bouncing or jumping being given.

POINTS TO OBSERVE
1. Although the heels must actually touch when one foot meets the other in First position, the contact must not be too hard.
2. There should be a slight slowing down of the step when a

41

change of direction is required. This is assisted by hands being held firmly, elbows slightly bent and down.
3. There are occasions when it is helpful to blend the last two slip steps of a movement into one step, in order to facilitate entry into the different step which follows (e.g. 'The Happy Meeting' (p.126), bars 17–24, where four slip steps are followed by pas de basque or skip change of step).

Running step

As the name implies, this is a natural running movement, one foot being lifted as the other is set down.

It is danced usually to 6/8 time (two steps to the bar) or 9/8 time (three steps to the bar).

Knees and feet face forward for this step.

Running step is danced on the ball of the foot, with the toes pointed down as much as possible, thus involving considerable ankle movement.

The step needs to be well controlled. To do so, the foot travelling forward should not be raised too high and is kept close to the foot carrying the weight. There must be no tendency to kick up behind on the change of weight from one foot to the other.

Strathspey

Strathspey travelling step

This is the travelling step which is the equivalent of skip change of step in reel and jig.

One strathspey travelling step takes one bar of music.

1. Reach forward with the right foot into Fourth position.
2. Close the left foot into Third position behind the right foot.
3. Reach forward again with the right foot into Fourth position.
4. Hop slightly on the right foot as the left foot is pulled through slowly from behind, ready to lead into the next step.

Rhythm: step, close, step-and-through.

Although the step has four parts in explanation, it can be seen that, in dancing it, parts three and four are blended into one continuous movement.

The character of strathspey travelling step is strong and dignified. Without being unnaturally stiff, the carriage of the body needs to be upright or the necessary balance will not be maintained. Although strong muscular control is required to dance the step well, the impression should be one of ease and smooth flowing elegance.

POINTS TO OBSERVE

1. The initial impetus of the front foot towards Fourth position is extended by a bend of the supporting knee and a flexible ankle. The foot is not 'placed' down in Fourth position but just reaches it when the weight is about to be transferred onto it.
2. When the feet are closed in Third position, the body itself is at its full height and the knees must be straight.
3. The second reach forward with the right foot, must be of sufficient length to leave the left leg fully extended in Fourth position behind.
4. With the knee turned out but not exaggerated, the rear foot is pulled slowly through with the toe just off the floor and the knee relaxing. Just as this rear foot passes the front foot, prior to straightening to start the next powerful urge forward, there is a very definite hop on the supporting foot, though that hop is kept low.

Strathspey travelling step is also used to travel backwards as in Advance and Retire. The movement is 'reach, close, reach-and-through'. In this instance the close is in Third position in front.

Strathspey setting step (common schottische)

This is equivalent to pas de basque in reel and jig.

One step takes one bar of music. In Scottish country dancing 'to set' means one setting step to the right and one to the left. It follows therefore, that 'to set twice' means four setting steps.

There are many similarities between strathspey travelling step and strathspey setting step but the latter is danced from side to side.

1. With the right foot, reach to the right into Second position.
2. Bring the left foot to Third position behind.
3. With the right foot, reach again to the right into Second position.
4. With a soft hop on the right foot, bring the left foot up behind the right leg, knee well turned out, toe just above the supporting heel and the side of the left foot against the back of the right leg.

The step is repeated to the left, with the left foot leading.

Rhythm: Step, close, step-and-hop.

As always, the posture must be good to maintain balance in this step and there should be no body turn to right or left when moving to the side.

POINTS TO OBSERVE

1. After the supporting leg has given a little to allow the urge of the initial extension, full height is regained in Third position.
2. The second reach into Second position must go far enough to leave the other leg well extended to the side, but not so far that balance and control are lost.
3. As the working foot is picked up from Second position to be placed behind the supporting leg at the end of the step, the

movement must be smooth and even with no drag along the floor, the line of knee and thigh being well maintained.

Viewed from the front, this working foot is hidden by the supporting leg.

As in the travelling step, the hop at the end of the step is a soft but positive lift.

4. Strathspey setting step may be used as a travelling step in certain movements where a limited distance is to be covered, such as Set Advancing and Poussette Right Round in Strathspey time. Instead of moving to Second position, the leading foot reaches to whatever other direction of travel is required for the formation. The other foot then closes in Third position. The leading foot again extends to travel as needed after which particular attention must be paid to complete the setting step correctly by lifting the working foot to behind the supporting leg at the end of the step.

In some dances, certain other steps may be used for setting in strathspey time. They are outwith the scope of these instructions, except for the Highland Schottische and the step used in 'The Glasgow Highlanders' (see p.122).

Highland Schottische

One Highland Schottische step takes two bars of music. In Scottish country dancing 'to set' with Highland Schottische means one step to the right and one to the left.

Each step has eight beats.

Beats 1, 2, 3, 4 are all danced on the spot, with a hop on the supporting foot on each beat.

Beats 5, 6, 7, 8 are the same as strathspey setting step.

1. Hop on the left foot, extend the right foot to Second position toe pointed down and touching the floor.
2. Hop on the left foot, lift the right foot and place it behind the

left leg, knee turned out, toe above heel.

3. Hop on the left foot, extend the right foot to Second position as in 1.

4. Hop on the left foot, lift the right foot to the front of the left leg, knee turned out, toe pointing down above the left ankle.

5. Reach with the right foot into Second position.

6. Close the left foot to the right foot in Third position behind.

7. Reach with the right foot into Second position.

8. Hop on the right foot, bringing the left foot up behind to place it behind the right leg, knee well turned out, toe above the supporting heel and pointing down.

The step is repeated with the left foot leading.

Rhythm: side, behind, side, in front, step, close, step-and-hop.

As this step is derived from the Highland dance tradition, it is acceptable in this step only for the men to place the foot against the supporting leg just below the knee on beats 2, 4 and 8. The appropriate Highland dance arm positions may be used.

The Glasgow Highlanders Step

This is the step associated with the dance of that name.

The step is used to give variety when eight bars of setting step are required in the dance.

The step itself takes two bars of music, therefore it needs to be danced 'right, left, right, left' to complete the eight bar phrase.

There are eight beats for each step.

1. Step forward onto the right foot as the left foot is lifted behind, knee turned out and toe pointing down.

2. Placing the left foot at the back of the right leg above the heel, hop on the right foot.

3. Step back onto the left foot as the right foot is raised in front, toe pointing down.

4. With the right foot raised in front of the left leg above the ankle, hop on the left foot.
5. Carry the right foot round behind the left leg and place it down behind the left foot, transferring weight to the right foot .
6. Step to the left with the left foot, transferring weight to the left foot.
7. Bring the right foot to the front of the left foot, transferring weight to the right foot.
8. Hop on the right foot as the left foot is lifted to the right leg, as in beat 1.
   Repeat to the other side with the left foot leading.

Rhythm: forward hop, backward hop, behind, side, in front, hop.

To contain both forward and sideways movement the steps should be small and neat. The hops should not be bouncy.

The body movement should be restrained, resisting any temptation to lean forwards or backwards.

FORMATIONS

General notes

1. Under the names of the individual formations, the following headings will be found:

   Steps: This indicates the type and number of steps to be used.

   Bars of music: This indicates the number of bars of music required to dance the formation.

   Hands: This indicates the manner in which the hands should be given and whether one or two hands are used.

2. Although the formations are divided into one or two bar

phrases for the purpose of description, the whole formation should be danced as a continuous, flowing movement.

3. All formations begin with the right foot unless otherwise stated.

4. When hands are given in a formation, they should be lifted, but not necessarily joined, at the beginning of the phrase.

Advance and Retire in reel, jig and strathspey time

This formation may be danced across or up and down the set or in dances round the room to vis-à-vis. There may be one, two, three or four couples involved. It is usually danced by dancers facing each other.

Hands: In lines of two or more couples, nearer hands are joined at shoulder height.

A. *Advance and Retire*

Steps: Four travelling steps.
Bars of music: Four.

Bars
1	One step forward with the right foot.
2	One step forward with the left foot. At the end of this step, the right foot is gently placed behind the left leg, with the toe pointed down just off the floor ready to begin the movement backward.
3	One step backward with the right foot.
4	One step backward with the left foot.

B. *Advance for one step and retire for one step in strathspey time*

Steps: Two travelling strathspey steps.
Bars of Music: Two.

Bars
1	One step forward with the right foot. At the end of this

48

step the left foot is brought up gently behind, close to the right heel ready to begin the movement backward.

2   One step backward with the left foot.

Note: Bars 1 and 2 are usually repeated, in which case at the end of bar 2 the right foot is brought in towards Third position, with the toe pointed down, just off the floor and continuing on into the next step forward.

Allemande in reel, jig and strathspey time

This formation is a method of progression.

Hands: The giving of hands in allemande is as follows:the man takes his partner's right hand in his right hand and her left in his left. He lifts her right hand over her head to hold it just above, but not resting on, her right shoulder. The man leads with his left hand. The timing of this movement depends on the previous formation in the particular dance and should be done smoothly.

Allemande for two couples

In this formation each man starts with his partner on his right.

Steps: Eight travelling steps.

Bars of music: Eight.

Bars

1   Starting from the middle of the set both couples dance a step diagonally to the right.

2   1st man wheels round bringing his partner beside him to face the man's side. 2nd couple follow.

3   1st couple dance a step across the dance and begin to turn down the man's side. 2nd couple follow.

4   1st couple dance a long step down the dance. 2nd couple follow into line of dance, also facing down.

5   Each man brings his partner round into a line facing the woman's side of the dance.

6   Both couples dance into the middle, each man bringing his partner round under her right arm to face him.

7   Releasing hands, both couples dance one step backward with the right foot.

8   Both couples dance one step backward with the left foot to finish on own side.
    (See Fig.)

Back to Back in reel, jig, and strathspey time

This formation is danced by two dancers facing each other.
Steps: Four travelling steps.
Bars of music: Four.

Bars
1 Dance one step forward with the right foot.
2 Passing right shoulder to right shoulder, dance one step with the left foot to pass each other back to back.
3 Passing left shoulder to left shoulder dance one step backward with the right foot.
4 Dance one step backward with the left foot to finish on the side line.

Balance in Line in reel and jig time

This formation is danced by three or four dancers in line facing alternate ways. It can be danced on the sidelines, across the dance or diagonally.
Steps: Two setting steps.
Bars of music: Two.
Hands: Nearer hands are joined at shoulder height.

Bars
1 Pas de basque right foot.
2 Pas de basque left foot.

Casting in reel, jig, and strathspey time

Casting can be a method of progression. In this case the standing couple/couples move up or down to vacate the place for the casting couple.

A. Cast off one place

Steps: Two travelling steps, beginning with the right foot
Bars of music: Two.

Bars
1   1st couple dance outward, the woman by the right and the man by the left.
2   1st couple dance down behind 2nd couple into second place.

B. Cast off one place

Steps: Four travelling steps, beginning with the right foot.
Bars of music: Four.

Bars
1   1st couple dance slightly in and up.
2   1st couple dance outward, the woman by the right and the man by the left.
3   1st couple dance down behind 2nd couple.
4   1st couple dance into second place.

C. Cast off two or three places

This is similar to cast off one place. When danced in two steps the 1st couple dance outward and down on bar 1. It is essential that the standing couples move up to shorten the track for the first couple.

When danced in four steps, the 1st couple dance slightly in on bar 1, and outwards and down on bar 2.

D. Cast up

This is similar to cast off. 1st couple dance outward, the woman by the left and the man by the right and dance up behind 2nd couple.

E. Cast off for four steps and cast up for four steps

This is similar to the other methods of casting off and casting up.

Bars
1   1st couple dance slightly in.

2   1st couple dance outward and down.

3–4   1st couple continue to dance down behind their own lines.

5   1st couple dance slightly down and outward, the woman by the left and the man by the right.

6–8   1st couple dance up to starting position.

F. Cross over and cast off

Steps: Four travelling steps.
Bars of music: Four.
Hands: Right hands are given with a shake-hand hold, at shoulder height

Bars

1–2   Giving right hands 1st couple cross into each other's place and face out.

3–4   1st couple continue dancing down behind 2nd couple into second place on opposite sides.

G. Turn and cast off

Steps: Four travelling steps.
Bars of music: Four.
Hands: Right hands are given with a shake-hand hold, at shoulder height.

Bars

1–2   Giving right hands 1st couple turn each other once round and dance out towards own side.

3–4   1st couple continue to dance out and down behind 2nd couple into second place.

H. Set and cast off

Steps: Two setting and two travelling steps.
Bars of music: Four.

Bars

1   Set on the right foot.
2   Still looking at partner, set on the left foot and begin to turn outward, the woman by her right and the man by his left.
3–4 Dance down behind 2nd couple into second place.

I. Set and cast up

Steps: Two setting and two travelling steps.
Bars of music: Four.

Bars

1   Set on the right foot.
2   Still looking at partner, set on the left foot and begin to turn outward, the woman by her left and the man by his right.
3–4 Dance up behind 2nd couple into first place.

Corner formations in reel, jig, and strathspey time

These formations are danced by three couples. The 2nd couple are in first place, the 3rd couple are in third place. The 1st couple stand back to back in the middle facing the opposite side: in this position first corners are on the 1st couple's right and second corners on their left. This means that for the first corner position, 1st woman faces 2nd man and 1st man faces 3rd woman so forming a diagonal line. For second corner position, the 1st woman faces 3rd man and 1st man faces 2nd woman, again forming a diagonal line.

A. Turn Corners and Partner in reel, jig and strathspey time

Steps: Eight travelling steps.
Bars of Music: Eight.
Hands: Hands are given at shoulder height with elbows down. A shake-hand hold is used.

Bars

1–2   1st couple turn first corners with the right hand.

3–4   1st couple turn each other with the left hand to face second corners.

5–6   1st couple turn second corners with the right hand.

7–8   Giving left hands, 1st couple cross to own side of the dance to finish in second place.

OP

TOP

First corner   *Second corner*

B. Set To and Turn Corners in reel, jig and strathspey time

Steps: In reel and jig time, eight setting steps. In strathspey time, two setting steps and two travelling steps for each corner.
Bars of music: Eight.
Hands: When turning, hands are joined at shoulder width and height.

Bars

1–2   1st couple set to first corners.

3–4   Giving both hands, 1st couple turn corners once round. First corners finish in place. 1st couple finish back to back in them middle of the set facing second corners.

5–6   1st couple set to second corners.
7–8   Giving both hands, 1st couple turn second corners. Second corners finish in place. 1st couple finish on the side lines between their corners.

C. Set to Corners in reel, jig and strathspey time

Steps: Four setting steps.
Bars of music: Four.

Bars
1   1st couple set to first corners.
2   1st couple, while setting on left foot to first corners, pull back the left shoulder as they begin to move round to face second corners.
3-4   1st couple set to second corners.

Note: The completion of this formation on bar 4 can differ from the above depending on the formation which follows.

D. Set to Corners and Partner in reel, jig and strathspey time

Steps: Eight setting steps.
Bars of music: Eight.

Bars
1   1st couple set to first corners.
2   1st couple, still setting to first corners, pull back the right shoulder to face partner. 1st couple are now on the side lines between their corners, facing partner across the dance.
3   1st couple set to each other.
4   1st couple, pulling back the right shoulder, dance into the middle of the set to finish back to back, facing second corners.

5	1st couple set to second corners.
6	1st couple, still setting to second corners, pull back the right shoulder to face partner. 1st man is now between 2nd couple facing down and 1st woman between 3rd couple facing up.
7–8	1st couple dance into second place on their own side, pulling back the right shoulder. In strathspey time, the seventh step can be modified to a travelling step.

Note: The completion of this formation can differ from the above depending on the formation which follows.

Cross Over in reel, jig and strathspey time

This formation is danced by one, two, three or four couples.
Hands: Partners give right hands at shoulder height in a shake-hand hold. The elbows are slightly bent.

A. Cross Over in two steps

Steps: Two travelling steps.
Bars of music: Two.

Bars
1	Giving right hands, dance one step to pass partner.
2	Releasing hands, dance out to opposite side, curving round by the right.

Note: This formation is usually preceded or followed by two setting steps.

B. Cross Over in four steps

Steps: Four travelling steps.
Bars of music: Four.

Bars
1	Raising the right hand, dance towards partner.

2   Giving right hand to partner, dance past each other.
3   Releasing hands dance out towards the opposite side.
4   Dance into opposite side line curving round by the right.

Double Triangles in reel and jig time

This formation is danced by three couples. To begin, the 2nd couple are in first place, the 3rd couple are in third place. The 1st couple stand closely back to back in the middle of the set, opposite second place and facing their own side of the dance.

Steps: Eight setting steps.

Bars of music: Eight.

Hands: When hands are given, it is with shake-hand hold at shoulder height to form a St Andrew's Cross. The arms are fully stretched but not rigid.

On bars 1 and 2, 1st woman gives right hand to 3rd woman and left hand to 2nd woman. 1st man gives right hand to 2nd man and left hand to 3rd man. On bars 5 and 6, hands are given similarly, 1st woman to 2nd and 3rd men and 1st man to 2nd and 3rd women.

Bars
   1–2   All set.
   3–4   1st couple move right about round each other to change places. 2nd and 3rd couples continue to set.
   5–6   All set.
   7–8   1st couple move right about round each other with springing pas de basque to finish on their own side in 2nd place. 2nd and 3rd couples continue to set.

Note: Depending on the size of the set, it may be necessary for the 2nd and 3rd couples to dance slightly in on bars 1 and 5 to give hands to 1st couple and then out again on bars 3 and 7. This allows the 1st couple to remain closely back to back throughout bars 1 to 6.

Bars 1 & 2   *Bars 5 & 6*

Figure of Eight in reel, jig and and strathspey time

This formation is danced by one couple.

Steps: Eight travelling steps.

Bars of Music: Eight.

A. Figure of Eight on the side line

Bars

1–8   1st couple face down. 1st woman dances behind 2nd
       woman and in front of 3rd woman curving by the left to
       face out just below the 3rd woman. She then dances up
       behind 3rd woman and in front of 2nd woman pulling
       back the left shoulder to finish in her original place. 1st
       man dances in front of 2nd man and behind 3rd man,

curving by the left to face in just below 3rd man. He then dances up in front of 3rd man and behind 2nd man, into is original place.

B. Figure of Eight Across the Dance

Bars
1–2   1st couple, woman passing in front of her partner, cross diagonally to opposite sides below 2nd couple and face out.
3–4   1st couple dance up behind the 2nd couple into partner's place.
5–6   1st couple, woman again passing in front of her partner, cross diagonally to own sides below 2nd couple and face out.
7–8   1st couple dance up behind 2nd couple into original place.

C. Figure of Eight for two couples (Double Figure of Eight)

In this formation both couples follow the pattern as described in Figure of Eight Across the Dance. On bars 1–2, 2nd couple dance up to top place to begin.

D. Half Figure of Eight Across the Dance and Half Double Figure of Eight

These are half of the previously described formations, danced with four steps to four bars of music.

Grand Chain in reel, jig and strathspey time

This formation is danced by three or four couples in a circular pattern. Dancers face clockwise and anti-clockwise alternately, continuing to dance round in this direction throughout the formation.

A. Grand Chain for three couples

Steps: Eight travelling steps.

Bars of music: Eight.

Hands: Hands are given at shoulder height with shake-hand hold, right and left given alternately.

  1st couple face across the dance.

  2nd couple face down the dance.

  3rd couple face up the dance.

Bars

1   1st couple pass each other giving right hand. 2nd woman and 3rd woman pass giving right hand. 2nd man and 3rd man pass giving right hand.

2   All pass the next dancer giving left hand.

3–4 All pass the next dancer giving right hand

5   All pass the next dancer giving left hand.

6   All pass next dancer giving right hand.

7–8 All pass the next dancer giving left hand.

Note: 1st man and 2nd woman finish the formation by pulling back the left shoulder (polite turn).

B. Grand Chain for four couples (eight steps)

Steps: Eight travelling steps.

Bars of music: Eight.

  1st and 4th couples face across the dance.

  2nd couple face down the dance.

  3rd couple face up the dance.

Bars

1   1st and 4th couples, 2nd and 3rd women and 2nd and 3rd men pass each other giving right hand.

2–8 Each dancer continues round giving left then right hand alternately, one step to each hand.

Note: 1st and 3rd men and 2nd and 4th women finish the formation by pulling back the left shoulder (polite turn).

C. Grand chain for four couples (sixteen steps)

Steps: Sixteen travelling steps.
Bars of music: Sixteen.

This is similar to the previously described formation, danced with sixteen steps to sixteen bars of music, two steps to each hand.

Hands Across in reel, jig, and strathspey time

This formation is often called a wheel, the hands in the centre forming the hub. The formation usually begins from the side lines.
Hands: Hands are given diagonally across the wheel in a shake-hand hold at shoulder height. The elbows are slightly bent.

A. Four Hands Across and Back

Steps: Eight travelling steps.
Bars of music: Eight.

Bars
  1–3   1st and 2nd couples dance on a curve to enter the wheel, and continue to dance round giving right hands across.
  4   All drop hands and turn inwards, by the right, to change direction.
  5–6   All give left hands across and dance round.
  7–8   Releasing hands, all dance out to finish on the side lines.

B. Four Hands Across Halfway Round (four steps)

Steps: Four travelling steps.
Bars of music: Four.

Bars
  1   1st and 2nd couples dance on a curve to enter the wheel.

2   Join right hands across and continue to dance round.
3   Release hands and dance towards new positions, i.e. 1st
     man to 2nd woman's place, 1st woman to 2nd man's
     place, 2nd man to 1st woman's place, 2nd woman to 1st
     man's place.
4   All curve round by the right to finish on the side lines.

C. Four Hands Across Halfway Round (two steps)

Steps: Two travelling steps.
Bars of music: Two.

Bars
1   1st and 2nd couples dance one long step in and round,
     giving right hands to form the wheel.
2   Releasing hands all dance out to new positions as in the
     previous formation.

Note: This formation is usually preceded or followed by two setting steps.

D. Six Hands Across and Back

Steps: Eight travelling steps.
Bars of music: Eight.
   This is the same formation as four hands across and back, but
is danced by three couples instead of two.

E. Three Hands Across

This formation requires three dancers and may be danced on the
side lines or across the dance.
Steps: Four travelling steps.
Bars of music: Four.
   This formation is the same as bars 1-4 of four hands across and
back, but the fourth step is used to link with the next movement.

Hands Round in reel and jig time

This formation always forms a circle and can be danced by three, four, six or eight dancers. The circular pattern is maintained throughout the formation. The circle is usually danced to the left and then to the right. All dancers begin with the LEFT FOOT.

Hands: As the circle is being formed hands are joined at shoulder height with the elbows slightly bent.

A. Hands Round and Back

Steps: Sixteen slip steps.
Bars of Music: Eight.

Bars

Bars	
1	Dancers moving on a curve, slip to the left and begin to join hands.
2–4	All continue dancing to the left. To prepare for the change of direction at the end of bar 4, the circle is slowed down and the heels are brought gently together.
5–6	All now slip to the right. At the end of bar 6, the dancers at the top and bottom of the circle release hands.
7–8	All continue to dance out on the curve to finish on the side lines.

B. Hands Round

Steps: Eight slip steps.
Bars of music: Four.

Bars

Bars	
1	Dancers moving on a curve, slip to the left and begin to join hands.
2	All continue dancing to the left. At the end of bar 2, the dancers at the top and bottom of the circle release hands.
3–4	All continue to dance out on the curve to finish on the side lines in starting place.

C. Hands Round Halfway

Steps: Eight slip steps.
Bars of music: Four.

Bars

1   Dancers moving on a curve slip to the left and begin to join hands.

2   All continue dancing to the left. At the end of bar 2, the dancers at the top and bottom of the circle release hands.

3–4 All continue to dance out on the curve to finish on the opposite side lines.

Hands Round in strathspey time

This formation always forms a circle and can be danced by three, four, six or eight dancers. The circular pattern is maintained throughout the formation. The circle is usually danced to the left and then to the right.
All dancers begin with the right foot.
Hands: As the circle is being formed, hands are joined at shoulder height with elbows slightly bent.

A. Hands Round and Back

Steps: Eight travelling steps.
Bars of music: Eight.

Bars

1   Dancers move on a curve to the left and begin to join hands.

2–4 All continue dancing to the left. At the end of bar 4 change direction.

5–6 All now dance to the right. At the end of bar 6 the dancers at the top and bottom of the circle release hands.

7–8 All continue to dance out on the curve to finish on the side lines.

B. Hands Round

Steps: Four travelling steps.
Bars of music: Four.

Bars

1   Dancers move on a curve to the left and begin to join
     hands.
2   All continue to dance to the left. At the end of bar 2
     dancers at the top and bottom of the circle release hands.
3–4 All continue to dance out on the curve to finish on the
     side lines in starting place.

C. Hands Round Halfway

Steps: Four travelling steps.
Bars of music: Four.

Bars

1   Dancers move on a curve to the left and begin to join
     hands.
2   All continue to dance to the left. At the end of bar 2
     dancers at the top and bottom of the circle release hands.
3–4 All continue to dance out on the curve to finish on the
     side lines on opposite sides.

Ladies' Chain in reel, jig and strathspey time

A. Ladies' Chain

This formation is danced by two couples. To begin, the 2nd couple are in first place and the 1st couple are in second place on the opposite sides.
Steps: Eight travelling steps.
Bars of music: Eight.
Hands: The hands are given at shoulder height with a shakehand hold.

Bars

1–2 1st and 2nd women, giving right hands, cross over to pass each other. At the same time, curving out to their right, 1st and 2nd men dance towards the woman's place.

3–4 Giving left hand, 1st and 2nd women turn their partners. The women finish diagonally opposite their starting place and the men finish back where they started, facing out.

5–6 Repeat bars 1 and 2.

7–8 Giving left hand, 1st woman turns 2nd man and 2nd woman turns 1st man, all finishing in their starting positions.

Note: 1st and 2nd men finish the final turn by pulling back the left shoulder (polite turn).

Start

Bars 1–2

67

B. Half Ladies' Chain

This is half of the previously described formation, danced with four steps to four bars of music.

Note: In some dances, the Ladies' Chain is danced with the woman beginning on the right of her partner.

Lead Down the Middle and Up in reel, jig and strathspey time

Steps: Eight travelling steps.
Bars of music: Eight.
Hands: The dancing couple join right hands. The man leads the woman with hands held about waist height.

A. Lead Down the Middle and Up

Bars
1–3   The dancing couple lead down the middle of the set.
4   They turn towards each other retaining right hands to face up.
5–7   They lead up the middle of the set and begin to dance out.
8   They dance diagonally out to original place.

B. Lead Down the Middle and Up followed by cast off

Bars
1–2   The dancing couple lead down the middle of the set.
3   They turn towards each other retaining right hands to face up.
4–6   They lead up to the top and begin to dance out.
7–8   They cast off to second place on own side. 2nd couple step up.

Petronella turn

By common usage, this is the name given to the turning movement within bars 1–16 of the dance 'Petronella' (see p.157).

Poussette in reel and jig time

This formation is a method of progression.

Hands: Hands are joined with partner at shoulder width and height, elbows down.

Note: This formation is danced with pas de basque.

Each man begins with his LEFT foot, each woman with her RIGHT.

A. Poussette for two couples

This formation begins with both couples side by side in the middle of the set. See Fig. overleaf.

Steps: Eight setting steps.

Bars of music: Eight.

Bars

1   Both couples dance one step away from the centre, 1st couple towards the man's side, 2nd couple towards the woman's side.

2   All dance a quarter turn, the men pulling with the right hand to finish on the side line, men facing down and women facing up.

3   All progress one step, 1st couple moving down the dance, 2nd couple up the dance.

4   All dance a quarter turn, men pulling with the right hand to finish facing own sides.

5   All dance one step into the centre.

6   All dance a half turn, men pulling with the right hand.

7–8 All dance backwards to own side line, having changed places.

B. Poussette in round-the-room dances

In round-the-room dances, one couple face another, the man with his partner on his right. Couples progress in the direction in which they originally faced.

Start position   *End of bar 1*

End of bar 2

End of bar 3

End of bar 4

End of bar 5   *End of bar 6*

(Pousette in round-the-room dances contd)

The formation begins with partners facing each other and with two hands joined.

Bars

1   Both couples dance one step in the direction in which the men are facing.

2   All dance a quarter turn, men pulling with the right hand.

3   All progress one step in the direction in which the women are facing.

4   All dance a quarter turn, men pulling with the right hand.

5   All dance one step in the direction in which the men are facing.

71

6   All dance a half turn, men pulling with the right hand.

7–8   Open out to face the next couple coming in the opposite direction.

C Poussette for one couple

As in 'The Triumph' (see p.177).

Poussette in strathspey time

This formation is danced by two couples.

Hands: Hands are joined with partner at shoulder height but held slightly wider than in the reel or jig poussette. The dance movements are long and sweeping and the hands are used to lead the steps.

Half Poussette

This formation is a method of progression. It begins with 1st and 2nd couples in a diagonal line, 1st woman and 2nd man back to back in the middle facing their partner. 1st couple are nearer the man's side and 2nd couple nearer the woman's side of the dance

Steps: Four setting steps.

Bars of music: Four.

Note: 1st woman and 2nd man begin with the *left* foot. 1st man and 2nd woman begin with the *right* foot.

Bars

1   1st couple dance diagonally out to the man's side and 2nd couple to the woman's side of the dance, both couples dancing a quarter turn by the right on the hop.

2   1st couple dance diagonally down and into the middle while 2nd couple dance diagonally up and into the middle, 1st man and 2nd woman passing back to back.

3   1st and 2nd couples, pulling with the right hand, turn to own side of the dance in the middle of the set.

4   1st and 2nd couples dance one step backward to own
     side line, having changed places. For this step only, the
     setting step is modified by bringing the foot into Third
     position in front.

Starting position   *End of bar 1*

End of bar 2

Promenade in reel, jig and strathspey time

This formation is danced by two, three or four couples. It usually begins in the middle of the set with the woman on the right of her partner.

73

Steps: Eight travelling steps.
Bars of music: Eight.
Hands: With hands crossed in front, right above left, the man takes his partner's right hand in his right hand and her left in his left. The arms are held away from the body, about waist height in the leading position. The man uses his right hand to lead.

A. Promenade for two couples

Bars
1	Both couples dance a step diagonally to the right.
2	1st man wheels round bringing his partner beside him to face the man's side. 2nd couple follow.
3	1st couple dance across the dance and turn down the man's side. 2nd couple follow.
4	Both couples dance down the man's side.
5	1st couple dance in towards the middle. 2nd couple follow.
6	1st couple dance up as 2nd couple dance in towards the middle.
7	Both couples dance up and begin to dance out.
8	Both couples dance diagonally out to original places.

B. Promenade for three couples

Bars
1	All three couples dance a step diagonally to the right.
2	1st man wheels round bringing his partner beside him and they dance across towards the man's side. 2nd and 3rd couples follow.
3	1st couple dance down the man's side. 2nd and 3rd couples follow.
4	1st couple continue to dance down the man's side. 2nd and 3rd couples follow.
5	1st couple dance in towards the middle and face up. 2nd and 3rd couples follow.

6   1st couple dance up as 2nd couple dance in towards the middle and face up. 3rd couple follows.

7   1st and 2nd couples continue to dance up as 3rd couple dance towards the middle and face up.

8   All three couples dance diagonally out to original places.

Note: When a three-couple promenade begins from the side lines, the first step is used to dance in to meet partner and face up.

Reels of Four in reel, jig and strathspey time

All reels of four are variations of the basic or ordinary reel of four. Reels of four can be danced on the side lines, across the dance or diagonally.

A. Basic Reel of Four on the side lines

The pattern of the reel danced by the four women is described below; the four men dance the same pattern at the same time.
Steps: Eight travelling steps.
Bars of music: Eight.
1st and 3rd women face down. 2nd and 4th women face up.

Bars
1   1st and 2nd women, and 3rd and 4th women, dancing to the left on a curve, pass right shoulders.

75

2   1st and 4th women pass left shoulders while 2nd woman dances up and round the loop to face down and 3rd woman dances down and round the loop to face up, both by the right.

3   2nd and 4th women, and 1st and 3rd women, pass right shoulders.

4   2nd and 3rd women pass left shoulders while 4th woman dances up and round the loop to face down and 1st woman dances down and round the loop to face up, both by the right.

5   4th and 3rd women, and 2nd and 1st women, pass right shoulders.

6   4th and 1st women pass left shoulders while 3rd woman dances upand round the loop to face down and 2nd woman dances down and round the loop to face up, both by the right.

7   3rd and 1st women, and 2nd and 4th women, pass right shoulders.

8   3rd and 2nd women pass left shoulders while 1st woman dances up to original place and 4th woman dances down to original place.

Note: To finish 1st woman pulls back the left shoulder and 3rd woman the right shoulder. To finish the reel of four on the man's side, 4th man pulls back the left shoulder and 2nd man the right shoulder.

B. Basic Reel of Four Across the Dance

This figure usually begins with 1st couple back to back in the middle of the dance, 1st woman facing 2nd man, 1st man facing 2nd woman. It finishes with both couples in starting positions. The figure follows the same pattern as the reel on the side lines but the 1st couple begin the reel by giving right shoulder to the person they are facing.

Steps: Eight travelling steps.
Bars of music: Eight.

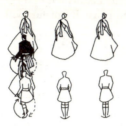

Bars

1   1st woman and 2nd man, and 1st man and 2nd woman, dancing to the left on a curve, pass right shoulders.

2   2nd couple pass left shoulders while 1st woman dances out and round the loop to face in and 1st man dances out and round the loop to face in, both by the right.

3   1st woman and 2nd woman, and 2nd man and 1st man, pass right shoulders.

4   1st couple pass left shoulders while 2nd woman dances out and round the loop to face in and 2nd man dances out and round the loop to face in, both by the right.

5   1st woman and 2nd man, and 1st man and 2nd woman pass right shoulders.

6   2nd couple pass left shoulders while 1st woman dances out and round the loop to face in and 1st man dances out and round the loop to face in, both by the right.

7   1st woman and 2nd woman, and 1st man and 2nd man pass right shoulders.

8   1st couple pass left shoulders while 2nd woman dances out and round the loop to face in and 2nd man dances out and round the loop to face in, both by the right. All are now back in starting positions.

C. Reel of Four Across the Dance starting from the side lines

This figure usually begins with 1st couple in top place and 2nd couple in second place. It finishes with both couples in starting positions.

Steps: Eight travelling steps.

Bars of music: Eight.

Bars

1 1st woman and 2nd man approach each other and pass left shoulders as 1st man and 2nd woman curve slightly to their left.

2 1st couple and 2nd couple pass partners right shoulders.

3 1st man and 2nd woman pass left shoulders while 1st woman dances out and round the loop to face in, and 2nd man dances out and round the loop to face in, both by the right.

4 1st woman and 2nd woman, and 1st man and 2nd man, pass right shoulders.

5 1st woman and 2nd man pass left shoulders while 2nd woman dances out and round the loop to face in, and 1st man dances out and round the loop to face in, both by the right.

6 1st couple and 2nd couple pass partners right shoulders and 1st woman and 2nd man dance out.

7 1st woman dances round the loop to face up and 2nd man dances round the loop to face down, both by the right. 1st man and 2nd woman pass left shoulders in the middle and dance out.

8 Passing right shoulders, 1st and 2nd women dance into original places, 1st woman curving by her right. Passing right shoulders, 1st and 2nd men dance into original places, 2nd man curving by his right.

Bar 1   Bar 8

D. Reel of Four Across the Dance, starting from the side lines and progressing one place

This figure usually begins with 1st couple in top place and 2nd couple in second place. It finishes with 1st couple in second place and 2nd couple in top place.

Steps: Eight travelling steps.

Bars of music: Eight.

Bars

1   1st woman and 2nd man pass left shoulders as 1st man and 2nd woman curve slightly to their left.

Bar 1

2   1st couple and 2nd couple pass partners right shoulders.

79

3   1st man and 2nd woman pass left shoulders as 1st woman dances out and round the loop to face in and 2nd man dances out and round the loop to face in, both by their right.

4   1st woman and 2nd woman, and 1st man and 2nd man, pass right shoulders.

5   1st woman and 2nd man pass left shoulders, as 2nd woman dances out and round the loop and 1st man dances out and round the loop, both by the right.

6   1st couple and 2nd couple pass partners right shoulders.

7–8   1st woman dances out and down to second place. 1st man and 2nd woman pass left shoulder. 1st man dances out to second place, pulling back his left shoulder, as 2nd woman dances out to top place, pulling back her left shoulder. 2nd man dances out and up to top place.

Bar 8

E. Diagonal Reel of Four

The pattern is similar to the basic reel of four across the dance. This figure usually begins with 1st couple back to back in the middle of the dance facing first corners, that is 1st woman faces 2nd man and 1st man faces 3rd woman. It finishes with all dancers in starting positions unless otherwise stated for a particular dance

Steps: Eight travelling steps.
Bars of music: Eight.

Bar 1

Bars

1   1st woman and 2nd man, and 1st man and 3rd woman, dancing to the left on a curve, pass right shoulders.

2   2nd man and 3rd woman pass left shoulders as 1st man dances out and round the loop to 3rd woman's place and 1st woman dances out and round the loop to 2nd man's place, both by the right.

3   1st woman and 3rd woman and 1st man and 2nd man, pass right shoulders.

4   1st couple pass left shoulders as 2nd man dances out and round the loop to 3rd woman's place and 3rd woman dances out and round the loop to 2nd man's place, both by the right.

5   1st woman and 2nd man, and 1st man and 3rd woman, pass right shoulders.

6   2nd man and 3rd woman pass left shoulders as 1st woman dances out and round the loop to 3rd woman's place and 1st man dances out and round the loop to 2nd man's place, both by the right.

7   1st woman and 3rd woman, and 1st man and 2nd man, pass right shoulders.

8   1st couple pass each other left shoulder to finish back to back in starting positions. 2nd man and 3rd woman curve by the right to finish in their starting positions.

F. Half Reel of Four

This is half the basic reel of four, danced with four steps to four bars of music.

Reels of Three in reel, jig and strathspey time

All reels of three are variations of the basic or ordinary reel of three. Reels of three can be danced on the side lines or across the dance.

A. Basic Reel of Three on the side lines

This figure is similar to a figure of eight on the side lines. The reel, if drawn on the floor, forms a figure of eight with well-rounded loops at each end.

The pattern of the reel danced by the three women is described below; the three men dance the same pattern at the same time.

Steps: Eight travelling steps.
Bars of music: Eight.
1st woman faces down. 2nd and 3rd women face up.

Bars

1   1st and 2nd women dancing to the left on a curve, pass
      right shoulders while 3rd woman curves to the right and
      dances up.

2   1st and 3rd women pass left shoulders while 2nd woman
      dances up and round the loop to face down.

3–4   2nd and 3rd women pass right shoulders while 1st
      woman dances down and round the loop to face up.

5   1st and 2nd women dancing to the right on a curve pass
      left shoulders while 3rd woman curves to the right and
      dances down.

6   1st and 3rd women pass right shoulders while 2nd
      woman dances down and round the loop to face up.

7–8   2nd and 3rd women pass left shoulders to finish in origi-
      nal places while 1st woman dances up to original place.

Note: to finish, 1st man and 3rd woman pull back the right
shoulder, and 3rd man and 1st woman the left shoulder.

B. Basic Reel of Three Across the Dance

This figure usually begins with 1st man between 3rd couple facing
3rd woman, and 1st woman between 2nd couple facing 2nd man.

   The figure follows the same pattern as the reel on the side
lines, but 1st couple begin the reel by giving right shoulder to
the person they are facing, that is 1st man to 3rd woman and 1st
woman to 2nd man, and they finish in the same position.

   The pattern of the reel danced by 1st woman with 2nd couple
is described below; 1st man and 3rd couple dance the same pattern at the same time.

Steps: Eight travelling steps.
Bars of music: Eight.

Bars

1   1st woman and 2nd man dancing to the left on a curve

83

pass right shoulders while 2nd woman curves to the right.

2   2nd man and 2nd woman pass left shoulders while 1st woman dances round the loop by her right.

3-4   1st and 2nd women pass right shoulders while 2nd man dances round the loop by his left.

5   1st woman and 2nd man dancing to the right on a curve pass left shoulders while 2nd woman dances round the loop by her right.

6   2nd man and 2nd woman pass right shoulders while 1st woman dances round the loop by her left.

7–8   1st and 2nd women pass left shoulders to finish in starting place while 2nd man dances round the loop by his right. All finish in starting places.

Note: when the basic reel begins by passing a *left shoulder* instead of a *right shoulder* as described in A and B above, the figure of eight pattern of the reel is still followed.

C. Reels of Three on Opposite Side and then On Own Side

These two reels are danced as one continuous movement. The pattern of the reels is the same as those already described, but the entry is different.

Steps: Sixteen travelling steps. (Eight steps for each reel.)

Bars of music: Sixteen.

1st couple face diagonally down. 2nd and 3rd couples face up.

Reel on opposite side

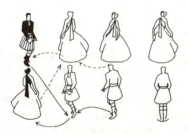

Reel on own side

Bars
1   1st woman, passing in front of her partner, crosses diagonally to second place to give left shoulder to 3rd man to begin the reel.

2–8   She continues as in the basic reel and finishes in her partner's starting place.

9   1st woman, again passing in front of her partner, crosses diagonally to second place to give right shoulder to 3rd woman to begin the second reel.

10–16 She continues as in the basic reel and finishes in her own starting place.

At the same time

Bars

1 1st man crosses diagonally to second place to give right shoulder to 3rd woman to begin the reel.

2-8 He continues as in the basic reel and finishes in his partner's starting place.

9 1st man crosses diagonally to second place to give left shoulder to 3rd man to begin the second reel.

10-16 He continues as in the basic reel and finishes in his own starting place.

At the same time

Bars

1–8 2nd couple curve outward and up to begin the reel. They continue as in the basic reel and finish in their own starting place, facing out and up. 3rd couple curve inward and up to begin the reel. They also continue as in the basic reel and finish in their own starting place facing in.

9–16 2nd and 3rd couples repeat bars 1–8 and finish in their own starting place.

On the last bar 2nd man pulls back his right shoulder and 2nd woman her left shoulder.

D. Reels of Three After Set To and Turn Corners

Reels of three following a formation which involves turning corners always begin with the 1st couple giving *left* shoulder to *first* corner.

The 1st couple are between their corners on the side line, facing their first corners.

The 2nd couple face down and 3rd couple face up.

The pattern of the reel danced by 1st woman and 2nd and 3rd men is described below; 1st man and 3rd and 2nd women dance the same pattern at the same time.

Steps: Eight travelling steps.

Bars of music: Eight.

Bars

1   1st woman and 2nd man pass left shoulders while 3rd man curves to his left.

2   1st woman dances round the loop by her left while 2nd and 3rd men pass right shoulders.

3   1st woman and 3rd man pass left shoulders while 2nd man dances round the loop by his right. At this point all dancers are exactly halfway through the reel.

4   1st woman and 2nd man pass right shoulders while 3rd man dances round the loop by his left.

5   1st woman dances round the loop by her right while 2nd and 3rd men pass left shoulders.

6   1st woman, passing 3rd man with the right shoulder, dances into the side line between her corners to face across the dance while 2nd and 3rd men dance into their starting positions, pulling back right shoulder and left shoulder, respectively.

7–8   Giving right hands, 1st couple cross over to their own side in second place.
      2nd and 3rd couples stand still.

E. Reels of Three After Set to Corners

Reels of Three following a formation which involves only *setting* to corners always begin with 1st couple giving *right* shoulder to *second* corner.

   1st couple are back to back in the middle of the set facing second corners.

   3rd couple face up and 2nd couple face down the dance.

   The pattern of the reel danced by 1st woman and 3rd and 2nd men is described below; 1st man and 2nd and 3rd women dance the same pattern at the same time.

Steps: Eight travelling steps.
Bars of music: Eight.

Bars

1   1st woman and 3rd man pass right shoulders while 2nd man curves to his right.

2   1st woman dances round the loop by her right while 3rd and 2nd men pass left shoulders.

3   1st woman and 2nd man pass right shoulders while 3rd man dances round the loop by his left. At this point all dancers are exactly half-way through the reel.

4   1st woman and 3rd man pass left shoulders while 2nd
      man dances round the loop by his right.
5   1st woman dances round the loop by her left while 3rd
      and 2nd men pass right shoulders.
6   1st woman, passing 2nd man with the left shoulder,
      dances into the side line between her corners to face
      across the dance while 3rd and 2nd men dance into their
      starting positions, pulling back left shoulder and right
      shoulder, respectively.
7–8   Giving right hands, 1st couple cross over to their own
      side in second place.
      2nd and 3rd couples stand still.

F. Reels of Three After Set to Corners and Partner

Reels of three following a formation which involves only *setting*
to corners and partner always begin with 1st couple giving *right*
shoulder to *second* corner.

  1st couple are back to back in the middle of the set facing second corners. On bar 8 of the previous formation, while still setting to their partner, they have danced towards each other
pulling back the right shoulder.

  This reel is then danced exactly as the previous formation (E).

G. Reels of Three After Turn Corners and Partner

Reels of three following a formation which involves *turning* corners and partner always begin with 1st couple giving *left* shoulder to *first* corner.

  1st couple are in the middle of the set. On bar 8 of the previous formation, 1st couple have guided each other with the left
hand towards their first corners so that 1st woman faces diagonally up towards 2nd man and 1st man diagonally down
towards 3rd woman.

  2nd couple face down and 3rd couple up the dance.

The pattern of the reel danced by 1st woman and 2nd and 3rd men is described below; 1st man and 3rd and 2nd women dance the same pattern at the same time.

Steps: Eight travelling steps.

Bars of music: Eight.

Start   *Bar 1*

Bars

1   1st woman and 2nd man pass left shoulders while 3rd man curves to his left.

2   1st woman dances round the loop by her left while 2nd and 3rd men pass right shoulders.

3   1st woman and 3rd man pass left shoulders while 2nd man dances round the loop by his right. At this point all dancers are exactly halfway through the reel.

4   1st woman and 2nd man pass right shoulders while 3rd man dances round the loop by his left.

5   1st woman dances round the loop by her right while 2nd and 3rd men pass left shoulders.

6   1st woman, passing 3rd man by the right shoulder, dances into the side line between her corners to face across the dance while 2nd and 3rd men dance into their starting positions, pulling back the right shoulder and left shoulder, respectively.

7–8   Giving right hands, 1st couple cross over to their own
       side in second place.
       2nd and 3rd couples stand still.

Rights and Lefts for two couples in reel, jig and strathspey time

This formation may be danced across or up or down the set or in
dances round the room and the pattern is that of a square.
Hands: Hands are given at shoulder height with a shake-hand
hold, the height of the hands being maintained as dancers pass
each other.

A. Basic Rights and Lefts

Partners face each other across the set.
Steps: Eight travelling steps.
Bars of music: Eight.

Bars
  1-2   1st and 2nd couples, giving right hand to partner, cross
        over to change sides.
  3-4   1st and 2nd women (on the man's side) and 1st and 2nd
        men (on the woman's side), giving left hand to each
        other, change places on the side lines.
  5-6   1st and 2nd couples, giving right hand to partner, cross
        over to change sides.
  7–8   1st and 2nd women and 1st and 2nd men, giving left
        hands to each other, change places on the side lines to fin-
        ish in their original places. On bar 8, 1st man and 2nd
        woman pull back the left shoulder (polite turn).

B. Half Rights and Lefts

This is half the previously described formation, danced with
four steps to four bars of music, 1st man and 2nd woman finishing with a polite turn.

Setting in Line in reel, jig, and strathspey time

This formation is danced by two, three, or four dancers facing the same direction. It may be danced across or up and down the set, or in dances round the room.

Steps: Setting steps as required.

Bars of music: One bar for each setting step. When Highland Schottische setting is used, two bars of music are required for each setting step.

Hands: Nearer hands are joined at shoulder height.

Stepping up or down in reel, jig, and strathspey time

This movement is used to leave a space for the dancing couple or to shorten the track over which they must dance. The step should be done with the heels off the floor.

Steps: Four even steps to four counts.

Bars of music: Two.

A. Stepping up

Count

1   Step up to the side with the foot nearer the top of the set.

2   Step across in front of it with the other foot.

3   Step up to the side again with the first foot.

4   Close the other foot into First position.

B. Stepping down

This is the same movement as stepping up, but begins with the foot nearer the bottom of the set.

Note: when two or more couples step up or down, they join nearer hands at shoulder height on the side lines. To assist a casting couple, it is helpful to step in and up on count 1 and back to the side line on count 3.

*Country Dances
Published by the
Royal Scottish
Country Dance
Society*

CIRCASSIAN CIRCLE

The dancers stand in fours, all round the room, each man having his partner on his right side, and another couple opposite, everyone dancing at the same time (see Fig.).

Bars   *(32 bar reel)*

1 – 8   Right and left. (bars 1 – 2) That is, the men give their right hands to the opposite women and cross over, changing places with them. (3 – 4) The men give left hands to their partners, and change places with them. The couples have now changed places. (5 – 8) Right and left again. The couples regaining their original places.

9 – 16   Set to partners, twice. Turn partners with both hands.

17 – 20   Ladies' chain. That is, women give right hands to one another, cross over and turn the opposite man round by the left hand. Men dance into partner's place to receive and turn opposite woman.

21 – 24   Repeat bars 17 – 20 but men turn own partners.

25 – 32   Poussette to change places with opposite couple thus progressing one place clockwise or counter clockwise.

Repeat, having passed a couple.

Note: this dance is the same as the first figure of Quadrille.
Source: collected locally and published in The Ballroom, 1827 *with a difference*

CLUTHA

Dancers arranged in square set as for Eightsome Reel.

Bars   *(48 bar reel)*

1 – 8   1st woman and 3rd man turn with right hands (2 skip change), dance round partner passing right shoulder (4 skip change) (Fig. 1), then turn each other again with right hand (2 skip change), remaining in the centre with right hands joined.

1

9 – 16   1st woman and 3rd man join left hand with partner and balance in line, then turn partner with left hand to finish 1st man and 3rd woman joining right hands in the centre, balance in line then turn partners back to original positions.

17 – 24   1st and 3rd couples dance rights and lefts.

25 – 32   1st and 3rd couples dance ladies' chain.

33 – 40   All turn corner with right hand (2 skip change), retaining right hands give partner left hand to form a circle (as in Fig. 2), all balance (2 pas de basque), then turn partner with left hand (4 skip change) to positions as in Fig. 3.

2

3

41 – 48 1st, 2nd, 3rd and 4th couples with promenade hold, dance round anti-clockwise to original positions.

Repeat three more times, the order to begin each turn being: 2nd woman and 4th man; 3rd woman and 1st man; 4th woman and 2nd man.

Source: Thomas Murphy's Aide Memoire (M.S.), c. 1890.
Strathclyde Regional Archives, Glasgow.

THE COLLEGE HORNPIPE

Bars   *(32 bar reel)*

1 – 8   1st, 2nd and 3rd couples dance six hands round and back again.

9 – 16   1st, 2nd and 3rd couples promenade (Fig.1).

1

17 – 24 1st couple, giving right hands, cross over, cast off one place, cross over giving left hands, cast off another place and lead up the middle to finish facing first corners. 2nd couple step up on bars 19 – 20.

25 – 32 1st couple set to first corners, then to each other across the dance, set to second corners, then clap and turn into own side line, one place down (Fig. 2).

2

Repeat, having passed a couple.

Source: Boag, 1797

COME UNDER MY PLAIDIE

Progressive round the room dance. The dancers stand
in fours, all round the room, each man having his
partner on his right side, and another couple opposite,
everyone dancing at the same time.

Bars   *(32 bar jig)*

1 – 4   All turn opposite partner with right hands (Fig 1).

1

5 – 8   All turn own partner with left hands to finish in promenade
         hold facing counter-clockwise, men on inside, women on
         outside.

9 – 16   Both couples promenade once round to original places
         (Fig. 2).

2

(see over)

17 – 24 Ladies' chain.

25 – 28 All joining nearer hand with partner, advance and retire.

29 – 32 All advance 3 skip change of step, passing opposite partner with right shoulder, then retire with 1 skip change of step.

Repeat having passed a couple.

Source: made available to the Society by Miss Jenny MacLachlan, by whom collected.

CUMBERLAND REEL

Bars   *(32 bar jig)*

1 – 8   1st and 2nd couples dance four hands across, giving right
              hands for four skip change of step, then giving left hands
              across dance back to original places.

9 – 16   1st couple lead down the middle and up again.

17 – 28   1st woman, turning to the right, cast off behind the women,
              while first man, turning to the left, casts off behind the men,
              the other men and women following, for six steps, then lead
              up the middle to places for six steps. On bar 28, 1st couple
              turn to face down, 2nd, 3rd and 4th couples join both hands
              with partners to make an arch.

29 – 32   1st couple dance down the middle under the arch (Fig.).
              On bar 32, 2nd, 3rd and 4th couples release hands and step
              back.

Repeat with a new top couple.

*Source: collected locally. 'The Cumberland' is mentioned as a country
dance early in the 19th century.*

101

THE DASHING WHITE SERGEANT

In groups of six round the room, one line of three facing another line of three. This can be danced with each line of three composed of a man between two women, or a man between two women facing a woman between two men (Fig.).

Bars   *(32 bar reel)*

1 – 8   Six hands round and back again.

9 – 12   The centre man or woman in each line of three, sets to and turns right hand partner with two hands.

13 – 16 The centre man or woman in each line of three, sets to and turns left hand partner with two hands.

17 – 24 Reels of three. The centre man or woman in each line of three begins the reel by passing right hand partner with the left shoulder.

25 – 28 With hands joined in original lines of three, advance and retire.

29 – 32 Each line of three advance through the opposite line of three, passing right shoulders with the dancer opposite, to meet the next line of three.

Repeat, with the next three dancers.

Source: attributed to David Anderson, Dundee (c.1897). Originally named La Danse Florence.

THE DE'IL AMANG THE TAILORS

Bars   *(32 bar reel)*

1 – 4   1st and 2nd couples with nearer hands joined on the sides, set to partners then dance four hands across half-way round with right hands.

5 – 8   Repeat bars 1–4 back to places, using left hands .

9 – 16   1st couple lead down the middle and up again.

17 – 24 1st and 2nd couples allemande (Fig.).

25 – 32 2nd, 1st and 3rd couples dance six hands round and back.

Repeat, having passed a couple.

Source: Davies Collection.

THE DUKE OF ATHOLL'S REEL

Bars   *(32 bar jig)*

1 – 4   With nearer hands joined, 1st and 2nd couples set and,
            giving right hands across, dance half way round.

5 – 8   Repeat bars 1–4 back to places, giving left hands across.

9 – 12   1st man and 2nd woman advancing, set to and turn each
            other with right hands (Fig. 1).

1

13 – 16 1st woman and 2nd man repeat bars 9 – 12.

17 – 20 1st couple, giving right hands, cross over and cast off one
            place on opposite sides. 2nd couple step up on bars 19 – 20.

21 – 24 1st couple dance half figure of eight round 2nd couple
            (Fig. 2 opposite).

25 – 32 2nd and 1st couples dance rights and lefts.

            Repeat, having passed a couple.

2

Source: Skillern 1776.

THE DUKE OF PERTH
(BROUN'S REEL)

Bars   *(32 bar reel)*

1 – 4   1st couple turn with right hands and cast off one place on own sides. 2nd couple step up on bars 3 – 4.

5 – 8   1st couple turn with left hands to face first corners.

9 – 10   1st couple turn first corners with right hands, i.e. 1st woman turns 2nd man, while 1st man turns 3rd woman.

11 – 12   1st couple turn with left hands to face second corners.

13 – 14   1st couple turn second corners with right hands, i.e. 1st woman turns 3rd man, while 1st man turns 2nd woman.

15 – 16   1st couple turn with left hands to face first corners.

17 – 20   1st couple set to and turn first corners, i.e. first woman sets to and turns 2nd man, while 1st man sets to and turns 3rd woman.

21 – 24   1st couple set to and turn second corners, i.e. 1st woman sets to and turns 3rd man, while 1st man sets to and turns 2nd woman.

25 – 30   Reels of three on the sides, 1st woman with 2nd and 3rd men, 1st man with 3rd and 2nd women (Fig. opposite).

31 – 32   1st couple cross over to own sides, in second place.

Repeat, having passed a couple.

Note: this dance is also known as 'Pease Strae'.

Source: The Ballroom, 1827.

THE EARL OF MANSFIELD

(48 bar reel)

1 – 8   1st and 2nd couple four hands round and back.

9 – 12   1st and 3rd couples face down, 2nd and 4th couples face up, all set and change places on the sides giving right hands.

13 – 16 2nd and 4th couples face down, 1st and 3rd couples face up, all set and change back to original places on the sides giving right hands. (2nd and 4th men stay facing out ready to dance out and up to enter reels of three).

17 – 24 1st man giving left shoulder to 2nd woman dances a reel of three across the dance with the second couple and collecting his partner with promenade hold on bar 20 continues the reel of three to finish in top place on the men's side.

3rd man dances similarly with the 4th couple to finish in third place on the men's side.

25 – 32 3rd couple dance into the centre and down between 4th couple, dividing they cast up to third place on opposite sides; giving right hands, they lead up between 2nd couple crossing over to own sides and cast off to original places.

1st couple following 3rd couple, dance into the centre and down between 2nd and 4th couples, dividing they cast up to third place on opposite sides; then they turn with the left hand to face first corners. 2nd couple step up bars 31 – 32.

33 – 36 1st couple turn first corners with the right hand, then pass one another with the right shoulder to face second corners. Corners dance four steps.

37 – 40 1st couple turn second corners with the left hand, then pass one another with the left shoulder to finish in the centre of the dance in second place facing up with nearer hands joined. Corners dance four steps.

41 – 44   1st man dances left hands across on the men's side with 2nd and 3rd men, while 1st woman dances right hands across on the women's side with 2nd and 3rd women. (At the end, as 1st couple dance in from third place, they touch nearer hands and dance down, 3rd couple follow 1st couple down the dance).

45 – 48   1st man dances right hands across with 3rd and 4th men, while 1st woman dances left hands across with 3rd and 4th women. (These wheels go round so that, at the end, 3rd couple dance up to second place, 4th couple dance up to third place, and 1st couple dance down to fourth place.)

Repeat, with a new couple.

Source: devised by John Drewry, 1980 and inscribed to William, Earl of Mansfield, President of the Royal Scottish Country Dance Society.

THE EIGHTSOME REEL

This is a square dance, danced by four couples.

Bars *(Reel)*

Part A

1 – 8   1st, 2nd, 3rd and 4th couples dance eight hands round to the left and back again to original places.

9 – 16   1st, 2nd, 3rd and 4th women dance four hands across with right hands, while retaining hold of partners with left hand. At the end of bar 12, women release right hands, 1st, 2nd, 3rd and 4th men, retaining hold of partners with right hands, move forward to change direction, then dance four hands across with left hands back to original places (Fig. 1).

17 – 24   1st, 2nd, 3rd and 4th couples set to partners twice, then turn partners once round with two hands, finish facing partners in original places.

25 – 40   1st, 2nd, 3rd and 4th couples dance a grand chain, i.e. they dance round the set giving right hand to partner to begin, then alternate hand to each man/woman they meet until they are all back in original places, when they face the centre. Two skip change of step are used for each hand given (Fig. 2).

2

Part B

1 – 8   1st woman moves into the centre of the dance and dances alone, while 1st man, 2nd, 3rd and 4th couples dance seven hands round to the left and back again.

9 – 16   1st woman sets to and turns partner with two hands, then sets to and turns 3rd man with two hands (Fig. 3).

3

17 – 24   1st woman, 1st and 3rd men, dance a reel of three, 1st woman begins the reel by giving left shoulder to 1st man. 1st woman stays in the centre at the end of the reel of three.

25 – 32   Repeat bars 1 – 8.

33 – 40   1st woman sets to and turns 4th man with two hands, then sets to and turns 2nd man with two hands.

(see over)

41 – 48 1st woman, 4th and 2nd men dance a reel of three, 1st woman begins the reel by giving left shoulder to 4th man. At the end of the reel of three, 1st woman resumes her original place in the dance and 2nd woman moves into the centre.

Repeat Part B, seven times, 2nd, 3rd and 4th women, then 1st, 2nd, 3rd and 4th men each having a turn in the centre.

Note:

1. In bars 1 – 8 and 25 – 32, the woman/man in the centre may dance any suitable reel steps.
2. In bars 9 – 16, the woman/man in the centre must always set to partner then man/woman on the opposite side of the dance.
3. In bars 33 – 40, the woman/man in the centre must always set to the man/woman on the right of her/his original position then man/woman on the opposite side of the dance. When all have had a turn in the centre, the dance finishes by repeating the whole of Part A.

It is said that this dance was produced by the late Earl of Dunmore and several friends, from their recollections of 'round reels'. They spent a week, in the early 1870s, evolving this dance at the time of the Atholl Gathering Ball. Later that season, or possibly the following year, it was introduced at the Portree Ball and at Perth. It caught on throughout the country and is now danced in all parts of Scotland. There are examples of round country dances to be found in old books, but none with quite the same figures. Tune: *The De'il Amang the Tailors.*

THE EXPRESS

1 – 8 1st woman dances reel of three with 2nd and 3rd men finishing in partner's place while 1st man does the same with 2nd and 3rd woman (Fig. 1).

1

9 – 16 1st, 2nd and 3rd couples dance reels of three on own sides (Fig. 2).

2

17 – 24 1st couple lead down the middle and up again.

25 – 32 1st and 2nd couples allemande, 1st couple finishing back to back ready for double triangles. On bars 31 – 32, 1st couple may use pas de basque as they open out to the top of the set to finish back to back for double triangles.

33 – 40 Double triangles (Fig. 3).

3

Repeat, having passed a couple.

Source: Button and Whittaker 1813.

THE FLOWERS OF EDINBURGH

Bars   *(32 bar reel)*

1 – 6   1st woman turns round by the right, and casts off two
places, i.e. dances down behind the 2nd and 3rd women,
then crosses over and dances up behind 3rd and 2nd men to
her partner's original position. (Fig.). At the same time, 1st
man follows his partner, crossing over and dancing behind
the 2nd and 3rd women, then up the middle to his partner's
original position.

7 – 8   1st couple set to one another.

9 – 14   Repeat bars 1 – 6, but 1st man leads, and 1st woman follows.
1st couple finish in original positions.

15 – 16 1st couple set to one another.

17 – 24 1st couple lead down the middle and up again.

25 – 32 1st and 2nd couples poussette.

Repeat, having passed a couple.

Source: collected locally. Published in The Ballroom, 1827.

THE FOULA REEL

1 – 8   1st couple lead down the middle and up again.

9 – 12   1st couple turn with right hands, then 1st man turns 2nd woman, while 1st woman turns 2nd man with left hands.

13 – 16   1st couple turn with right hands, then 1st man turns 3rd woman while 1st woman turns 3rd man with left hands.

17 – 20   Repeat bars 13 – 16 with 4th couple.

21 – 24   1st couple cast up to the top behind their own line.

25 – 28   2nd, 3rd and 4th couples kneel down and clap, while 1st couple, with nearer hands joined, dance down, one on each side of women's line, and up, one on each side of men's line. (Fig. 1)

1

29 – 40   1st, 2nd, 3rd and 4th couples join two hands with partners and move forwards and backwards; 1st couple dance in and out between 2nd, 3rd and 4th couples until they reach the bottom of the set. 1st couple move out to the men's side and back to the centre, while 2nd, 3rd and 4th couples move out to the women's side and back to the centre. (Fig. 2)

2

Repeat, with a new top couple.

Running step (see p. 42) is used throughout the dance – two steps to each bar of music.

Source: tune and dance collected in Shetland.

FOURSOME REEL

A complete strathspey and reel set consists of two couples who start the dance facing each other. The men have their partners on their right as in Fig. 1.

TOP

1

Bars *(Medley)*

Strathspey

1 – 8   Both couples describe a Reel of Four across the room (Fig. 2), finishing as in Fig. 3.
Note: In starting the dance the men wait two bars while the women pass left shoulders in the centre.

2   3

9 – 16   All Set.

17 – 24   Repeat Reel of Four, finishing as in Fig. 4.

4

25 – 32   All set.

This dance may be repeated as often as desired. The usual number is four times Reel of Four and four strathspey setting steps.

Reel
1 – 32   Danced as above but in reel time with reel steps.

Note: the Reel should be repeated the same number of times as the Strathspey. The number of times should be a multiple of two so that dancers will finish in original places and with own partners.

GENERAL STUART'S REEL

Bars   *(32 bar reel)*

1 – 4   1st man sets to 2nd woman and casts off one place, 2nd man steps up on bars 3 – 4.

5 – 8   1st woman sets to 2nd man and casts off one place, 2nd woman steps up on bars 7 – 8.

9 – 10   1st man turns 3rd woman with right hand while 1st woman turns 2nd man with right hand (Fig. 1).

1

11 – 12   1st couple, passing right shoulders, face second corners (Fig. 2).

2

13 – 16 1st man turns 2nd woman by left hand while 1st woman turns 3rd man by left hand, passing each other right shoulder to face first corners.
Note: on bars 9–16, corners dance two steps when turning.

17 – 20 1st couple set to first corners, then to each other across the dance.

21 – 24 1st couple set to second corners, then to each other up and down dance. (Turn to right throughout.)

25 – 30 Reels of three at the sides. 1st couple begin the reel by giving right shoulders to second corner (Fig. 3).

3

31 – 32 1st couple cross over to own sides one place down.

Repeat, having passed a couple.

Source: Castle Menzies MSS, 1749

THE GLASGOW HIGHLANDERS

On the second chord, 1st woman crosses over to the right hand side of her partner. 2nd man takes his partner's place while she moves up to the top (Fig. 1).

1

Bars   *(32 bar strathspey)*

1 – 8   1st and 2nd couples dance rights and lefts, giving right hand to dancer opposite to begin. On bar 7, 2nd man gives his left hand to his partner and dances diagonally down into the middle, offering his right hand to 1st woman, who has been handed over to him by 1st man.

9 – 12   2nd man between 1st and 2nd women, with hands joined, dance down the middle followed by 1st man (Fig. 2). Release hands, all turn to face top, 2nd man turning 1st and 2nd women towards him, while 1st and 2nd men turn right about.

2

13 – 16   1st man gives left hand to his partner and right hand to 2nd woman, all three dance up the middle, 2nd man following. Finish at the top in a line of four across the dance and facing partner, men back to back in the middle, women on the side lines.

17 – 24   1st and 2nd couples set to partner with simple Strathspey steps (see p. 46) (Fig. 3).

3

25 – 32   1st and 2nd couples dance a reel of four across the dance. On bars 31 – 32, 1st woman progresses down to third place on men's side of dance, 1st man follows, progressing to second place, 2nd man dances round 1st man, passing left shoulders, to top place on men's side of dance, 2nd woman dances to top place on women's side of dance. 3rd woman steps up to second place and 3rd man moves across to his partner's original place (Fig. 4).

4   (see over)

Repeat, having passed a couple.

Note: each man, having in turn crossed to the side of his partner, stays on the woman's side of the dance until he reaches the top. He and his partner then stand still on their own sides for one turn, at the end of which the woman crosses over to her partner's right hand side, and they dance all the way down on the men's side. At the bottom, each couple stands on own sides for one turn before the man crosses over to his partner to progress up to the top again.

Bars 7 – 8: As 2nd man gives left hand to his partner on bar 7 he must dance diagonally into the centre of the dance, while 2nd woman dances left about to finish facing down the set, her right hand in her partner's left. At the same time, as 1st couple give left hand, 1st man dances diagonally into the centre to finish behind 2nd man, also facing down. He hands 1st woman in to finish with her left hand in the right hand of 2nd man.

Bar 16: 2nd man must dance up to finish back to back with 1st man in a line of four across the dance. 1st woman is now in 2nd man's original place and 2nd woman is in her own place. This must be done to ensure that the set does not move gradually up the room.

Bars 25 – 32: The reel of four must be completed in six steps to leave the last two bars for the progression. The progression is made by 1st couple dancing down the man's side ready to face 3rd couple, 3rd man having crossed over and 3rd woman having stepped up. 2nd couple finish in top place on their own sides.

Source: W. F. Gillies Manual of Dancing or A Complete Companion to the   Ballroom, *Glasgow, c. 1885.*

HAMILTON HOUSE

Bars   *(32 bar jig)*

1 – 4   1st woman advancing, sets to 2nd man, then turns 3rd man, and stands between them.

5 – 8   1st man advancing, sets to 2nd woman, then turns 3rd woman, and finishes between 3rd couple, while 1st woman moves up between 2nd couple, who also move up on bars 7 – 8.

9 – 12   1st, 2nd and 3rd couples with nearer hands joined, set twice across the dance (Fig. 1).

13 – 16   1st couple, with both hands, turn each other three-quarters round to finish in 2nd place on opposite sides.

17 – 20   2nd, 1st and 3rd couples set twice on the sides.

21 – 24   1st couple turn each other half-way round with two hands to finish on own sides in second place.

25 – 32   2nd, 1st and 3rd couples dance six hands round and back again (Fig. 2).

Repeat, having passed a couple.

1   2

Note: pas de basque step is used throughout except for the last eight bars.
Source: William Campbell's Fourth Collection, c. 1789.

THE HAPPY MEETING

1 – 8   1st man and 2nd woman passing right shoulders in the middle dance a figure of 8 round the 1st woman and 2nd man (Fig. 1).

1

9 – 16   1st woman and 2nd man passing left shoulders in the middle dance a figure of 8 round the 1st man and 2nd woman (Fig. 2).

2

17 – 20   1st couple dance 4 slip steps down the middle and set to each other.

21 – 24   1st couple dance 4 slip steps up the middle and cast off into second place. 2nd couple step up on bars 23 – 24.

25 – 28   2nd and 1st couples advance and retire; all clap at the end of bar 28.

29 – 32   2nd and 1st couples turn partners with right hands.

Repeat having passed a couple.

Source: traditional.

THE HAYMAKERS

Bars *(48 bar jig)*

1 – 4   1st woman and 4th man advance to the middle of the dance, turn with right hands and return to original places (Fig. 1).

1

5 – 8   1st man and 4th woman repeat bars 1 – 4.

9 – 12   1st woman and 4th man repeat bars 1 – 4 but turn with left hands.

13 – 16   1st man and 4th woman repeat bars 9 – 12.

17 – 20   1st woman and 4th man repeat bars 1 – 4 but turn with two hands.

21 – 24   1st man and 4th woman repeat bars 17 – 20.

25 – 28   1st woman and 4th man advance and dance back to back, passing right shoulders without taking hands, then pass left shoulders and retire to original places.

29 – 32   1st man and 4th woman repeat bars 25 – 28.

33 – 36   1st woman and 4th man advance, curtsey or bow to one and other and retire to original places.

37 – 40   1st man and 4th woman repeat bars 33 – 36.

41 – 44   1st woman casts off to fourth place followed by 2nd, 3rd and 4th women, while 1st man casts off followed by 2nd, 3rd and 4th men. 1st couple meet in the middle and join hands to form an arch (Fig. 2).

2

45 – 48   2nd, 3rd and 4th couples dance up the middle under the arch.

Repeat, with a new top couple.

Note: running step (see p. 42) is used throughout.
Source: traditional.

THE HIGHLAND FAIR

Bars *(32 bar jig)*

1 – 8   1st couple cast off behind own lines and then cast up to place.

9 – 16   1st and 2nd couples turn partners with the right hand and then with the left hand.

17 – 20   1st couple, followed by 2nd couple, lead down the middle (Fig. 1).

21 – 24   2nd couple, followed by 1st couple, lead up again (Fig. 2). 2nd couple finish in first place and 1st couple finish in second place.

25 – 32   2nd and 1st couples dance rights and lefts.

Repeat, having passed a couple.

Source: The Lady's Companion or Complete Pocket Book for the Year 1801.

HOOPER'S JIG

1 – 4   All clap and 1st couple cross over, passing right shoulders and cast off one place on the opposite side of the dance. 2nd couple step up on bars 3 – 4.

5 – 8   1st and 3rd couples dance right hands across right round for 4 skip change of step.

9 – 16   All clap and 1st couple cross over passing right shoulder, cast up to own places and dance left hands across with 2nd couple right round to place. 2nd couple step down on bars 11 – 12.

17 – 18   1st man giving right hand to 3rd woman, dances across to change places with her.

19 – 20   1st woman giving right hand in passing, crosses over with 3rd man while 1st man and 3rd woman dance round ready to cross over again.

21 – 22   1st man and 3rd woman giving right hand cross over to own place while 1st woman and 3rd man dance round ready to cross.

23 – 24   1st woman and 3rd man giving left hand, cross over but 3rd man guides 1st woman into 2nd place while 1st man casts off round 2nd man into 2nd place – 2nd couple having moved up (see Fig. overleaf).
Note: left hand is given once only when 3rd man has to guide 1st woman into 2nd place.

(see over)

25 – 32   2nd and 1st couples dance rights and lefts.

1st couple repeat dance with next two couples.

Source: traditional.

INVERNESS COUNTRY DANCE
(SPEED THE PLOUGH)

Bars   **(32 bar reel)**

1 – 8   1st and 2nd couples dance four hands across giving right hands and back again giving left hands (Fig. 1).

9 – 16   1st couple lead down the middle and up again to finish facing first corners. 2nd couple step up on bars 11–12.

17 – 20 1st couple set to and turn first corners, finishing facing second corners.

21 – 24 1st couple set to and turn second corners, finishing 1st woman between 2nd couple facing down, 1st man between 3rd couple facing up (Fig. 2).

25 – 32 1st couple set to each other twice, then turn with two hands one and a quarter times to own sides of dance in second place.

Repeat, having passed a couple.

1   2

Source: collected in Inverness-shire.

JOHNNY GROAT'S HOUSE

(32 bar reel)

1 – 4   1st couple with both hands joined, slip 4 steps down the middle between 2nd couple, and 4 steps up again (Fig. 1).

1

5 – 8   1st couple cast off one place, meet in the middle and join both hands. 2nd couple step up on bars 7 – 8.

9 – 16   1st couple repeat bars 1 – 8 with 3rd couple, and finish in third place.

17 – 24   2nd, 3rd and 1st couples dance six hands round and back again.

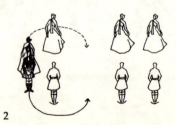

2

25 – 32 1st couple with 4 steps lead up to the top, set and cast off into 2nd place. 3rd couple move down (Fig. 2).

Repeat, having passed a couple.

Source: Rutherford 1748.

La Russe

This is a square dance for 4 couples. The dance is repeated 3 times till each couple has had a turn as leading couple.

Bars   *(Reel)*

1 – 2   Using two setting steps, all change places with partners to face their partner's corner position; men passing their partners in front of them with the right hand (Fig.).

1

3 – 4   All set.

5 – 8   All turn the person in partner's corner position with both hands to finish facing own partners.

9 – 16 All set twice to partners, and turn with both hands one and a half times to finish in original places.

17 – 24 1st man leads his partner by the right hand in a promenade anti-clockwise round the set, back to original places facing in.

25 – 32 1st couple poussette round inside the set, back to original places facing in.

33 – 40   1st and 3rd couples change places, the 1st couple dancing between the 3rd couple. They cross back with the 3rd couple dancing between 1st couple (Fig. 2).

2

41 – 48   1st and 3rd couples repeat bars 33 – 40.

49 – 56   All dance eight hands once round to the left.

57 – 64   With the men giving nearer hand to partners, the women join right hands across and all dance once round to finish in original places.

The dance is then repeated with, in turn, the 2nd, 3rd and 4th couple leading.

Note regarding the pousette: this movement starts with 1st couple facing each other, in place, with both hands joined. The man starts on his left foot, the woman on her right.

Bar
1–2   Dance 1 step towards the 4th couple's side and quarter turn by the right.
3–4   Dance 1 step towards the 3rd couple's side and quarter turn by the right.
5–6   Dance 1 step towards the 2nd couple's side and quarter turn by the right.
7–8   Dance 1 step towards own side and quarter turn by the right.

Source: as danced in Forfar.

LA TEMPÊTE

The couples stand in fours across the room, two couples facing two couples, women on the right of their partners (Fig.).

TOP

Bars   *(48 bar reel)*

1 – 8   1st and 4th couples dance four hands across with right hands and back again with left hands.

9 – 16   2nd and 3rd couples repeat bars 1 – 8.

17 – 24   1st, 2nd, 3rd and 4th couples set twice and turn partners with two hands.

25 – 28   1st, 2nd, 3rd and 4th couples join both hands with partner and slip across to change places with opposite couple, i.e. 1st with 3rd and 2nd with 4th, men passing back to back.

29 – 32   1st, 2nd, 3rd and 4th couples repeat bars 25 – 28 back to places, women passing back to back.

33 – 36   1st and 3rd couples and at the same time 2nd and 4th couples, dance four hands round to the left.

37 – 40   1st and 3rd couples and at the same time 2nd and 4th couples, dance four hands across (left hands) back to original places.

41 – 43   1st, 2nd, 3rd and 4th couples advance two steps and retire one step.

44   1st, 2nd, 3rd and 4th couples clap three times.

45 – 48   1st and 2nd couples dancing down the dance, pass under the raised arms of 3rd and 4th couples, who are dancing up. Repeat with the next two couples and dance the same figures with every line until they arrive at the bottom of the room. As each line reaches the top or bottom of the room, change to correct side of partners and stand during one turn of the dance.

Note: this dance can also be done in groups of four in a circle, in which case, bars 9 – 16 are omitted.

Source: collected locally.

LADIES' FANCY

Bars   **(32 bar jig)**

1 – 4   1st man turns 2nd woman with right hands and returns to place.

5 – 8   1st man turns 1st woman with left hands one and a half times to finish facing down the dance with 1st woman on his right side and 2nd woman on his left (Fig.). 2nd woman steps up on bars 7 – 8.

9 – 16   They lead down the middle and as they lead up 1st man hands his partner across in front of him to finish on own sides at top.

17 – 24   1st and 2nd couples four hands across and back.

25 – 32   1st and 2nd couples poussette.

Repeat, having passed a couple.

Note:
Bars 5 – 8:   When 1st man turns 1st woman with left hand to finish facing the bottom of the dance with her on his right hand, it is very helpful to join both hands on bars 7 – 8, bringing 1st woman on to his right hand,

having turned a full turn in doing so. 2nd woman
steps up on bars 7 – 8.

Bars 15 – 16:   On coming up the middle on bars 15 – 16, 1st man
brings his partner round to her own side of the
dance and hands her right hand to 2nd man who
has come in behind him to receive it. 2nd woman
quickly changes her hand and the wheel is formed.

Source: collected in Angus.

LAMB SKINNET

Bars   *(32 bar jig)*

1 – 4   1st couple set and cast off to second place. 2nd couple step up on bars 3 – 4 (Fig.).

5 – 8   1st couple dance a half figure of eight round 2nd couple finishing in second place on opposite sides.

9 – 12   1st couple set and cast off to third place. 3rd couple step up on bars 11 – 12.

13 – 16   1st couple dance a half figure of eight round 3rd couple finishing in third place on own side.

17 – 24   1st couple lead up the middle to first place, set and cast off into second place. 3rd couple step down on bars 19 – 20. 2nd couple step up on bars 23 – 24.

25 – 32   2nd and 1st couples dance rights and lefts.

              Repeat, having passed a couple.

Source: Thompson, 1751

THE LEA RIG

Bars   **(32 bar strathspey)**

1 – 16   1st couple dance the first figure of Petronella. 2nd couple, joining in on third bar, set, then they turn following the 1st couple one place behind. On the last two bars instead of setting, the 2nd couple turn to their original places. 2nd couple step up on bars 1 – 2.

Bars 9 – 10

17 – 24   1st couple lead down the middle and up again.

25 – 28   1st and 2nd couples, giving right hands, dance four hands across right round.

29 – 32   1st and 2nd couples half poussette.

          Repeat, having passed a couple.

Source: collected from an old MS.

LINTON PLOUGHMAN

Bars

1 – 8   1st and 2nd couples dance four hands round to the left and back again (Fig. 1).

1

9 – 16   1st and 2nd couples dance four hands across with right hands and back again with left hands.

17 – 24   1st couple lead down the middle and up again (Fig. 2).

2

25 – 32   1st and 2nd couples poussette.

Repeat, having passed a couple.

Source: collected in Peebles-shire.

THE MACHINE WITHOUT HORSES

Bars

(32 bar jig)

1 – 4 1st couple set and cast off one place. 2nd couple step up on bars 3 – 4.

5 – 8 1st and 3rd couples dance right hands across, once round.

9 – 12 1st couple set and cast up to the tope. 2nd couple step down on bars 11 – 12.

13 – 16 1st and 2nd couples dance left hands across, once round.

17 – 24 1st couple, followed by the 2nd couple, lead down between 3rd couple, divide, and cast up round them. Lead up to the top, and then cast off to second place while 2nd couple dance into the top place (Fig). 1st and 2nd couples give nearer hands when leading.

25 – 32 2nd and 1st couples dance rights and lefts.

Repeat, having passed a couple.

Source: Rutherford, 1772.

MAXWELL'S RANT

Bars

(32 bar reel)

1 – 8   1st woman dances a reel of three with 2nd and 3rd men finishing in her partner's place, while 1st man does the same with 2nd and 3rd woman (Fig.).

9 – 16   1st, 2nd and 3rd couples dance reels of three on own sides.

17 – 20   1st couple giving right hands, cross over and cast off one place. 2nd couple step up on bars 19 – 20.

21 – 24   1st couple dance half a figure of eight round 2nd couple.

25 – 28   1st couple lead down between 3rd couple and cast up into second place.

29 – 32   2nd, 1st and 3rd couples turn partners with right hands.

Repeat, having passed a couple.

Source: Rutherford 1752.

MIDDLING, THANK YOU

Bars *(40 bar jig)*

1 – 8   1st and 2nd couples set twice then dance half rights and lefts (to change sides and places) (Fig. 1).

1

9 – 16   Repeat back to places.
             On bar 16, 2nd woman and 1st man complete the polite turn of the half right and left as they dance in for the poussette.

17 – 24   1st and 2nd couples poussette.

25 – 32   1st couple lead down the middle, up again to the top and cast off one place round 2nd couple. Finish facing corners (Fig. 2).

2

(see over)

33 – 40   1st couple turn first corners with right hands, partner in the middle with left hand, second corner with right hand, then, giving partner left hand, cross to own sides, one place down.

Repeat, having passed a couple.

Source: Button and Whitaker 1812.

THE MONTGOMERIES' RANT

Bars *(32 bar reel)*

1 – 4   1st couple giving right hands, cross over and cast off one place, 2nd couple step on bars 3 – 4.

5 – 8   Cross over again, giving left hands, and the woman casts up one place and the man casts down one place (Fig. 1).

1

9 – 16   Reels of three across the dance (Fig. 2).

2

17 – 18   1st couple taking nearer hands set to 2nd woman, change hands and

19 – 20   Set to 3rd man.

(see over)

21 – 22 Set to 3rd woman, change hands and

23 – 24 Set to 2nd man.

25 – 30 Reels of three at the sides. 1st couple begin the reels by giving right shoulder to second corner (Fig. 3).

3

31 – 32 1st couple cross over to own sides in second place.

Repeat, having passed a couple.

Source: Castle Menzies MSS., 1749.

MONYMUSK

(32 bar strathspey)

1 – 4   1st couple turn with right hands and cast off one place. 2nd couple step up on bars 3 – 4.

5 – 8   1st couple turn with left hands one and a quarter times to position as in Fig 1.

1

9 – 12   Set three and three twice. On bars 11 – 12, 1st couple turn to their right, finishing as in Fig. 2.

2

13 – 16   Set three and three twice.

17 – 24   2nd, 1st and 3rd couples six hands round and back.

25 – 30   Reels of three at the sides. 1st couple begin the reel by giving right shoulder to the person on their right (Fig. 3).

(see over)

3

31 – 32   1st couple cross to own sides in second place.

Repeat, having passed a couple.

Source: Preston, c. 1786.

MRS. MACLEOD

Bars (32 bar reel)

1 – 8   1st and 2nd couples dance four hands across and back again.

9 – 16   1st couple lead down the middle and up again to face corners. 2nd couple step up on bars 11 – 12 (Fig.).

17 – 24   1st couple set to and turn corners.

25 – 30   Reels of three at the sides.

31 – 32   1st couple cross to own sides in second place.

Repeat, having passed a couple.

Source: The Ballroom, or the Juvenile Pupil's Assistant, 1827.

MY LOVE SHE'S BUT A LASSIE YET

Two chords. On the second chord, 1st couple cross over
to positions as in Fig.

Bars   **(32 bar reel)**

1 – 4   1st woman and 2nd man set and then change places with two skip change of steps, passing right shoulders. At the same time the 1st man and 2nd woman set and change places.

5 – 8   2nd and 1st couples set to partner then cross over to change sides, passing right shoulders.

9 – 16   Repeat to bars 1 – 8.

17 – 24 1st and 2nd couples dance four hands round twice, finishing as in Fig. but facing partner.

25 – 32 1st and 2nd couples poussette. 1st couple finish as in Fig. but facing the 3rd couple with whom they repeat the dance.

Note: in the poussette the 1st couple begin and end on the opposite sides of the dance. As couples reach the bottom of the dance they return to own sides. This dance may also be done round the room in circular formation.

Source: collected in Perthshire.

NEIDPATH CASTLE

(32 bar strathspey for 3 couples)

1 – 2   All three couples set to partners.

3 – 6   All three couples, giving both hands, turn partners twice.

7 – 8   All three couples set again to partners.

9 – 16   Grand chain (Fig. 1).

1

17 – 24   1st couple, with nearer hands joined, dance between the 2nd couple, behind the 3rd couple and up between the third couple; 1st couple dance up behind 2nd couple and finish at the top with hands joined ready to dance half poussette with 2nd couple who dance in on bar 24.

25 – 28   1st and 2nd couples dance a half poussette, 2nd couple finishing in the top place while 1st couple turn in the middle. 3rd couple dance in on bar 28 to join 1st couple (Fig. 2).

2

(see over)

29 – 32 1st and 3rd couples dance a half poussette, 1st couple finishing in 3rd place.

Repeat, with a new couple leading each time.

Source: devised by Derek Haynes, Liverpool Branch, RSCDS.

PETRONELLA

Bars   *(32 bar reel)*

1 – 2   1st woman moves from A to B with two pas de basque steps, leading off with the right foot and making a three-quarter turn, in the middle of which she has her back to her partner. 1st man moves similarly from C to D.

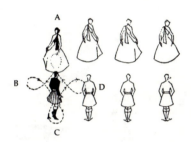

3 – 4   1st couple face each other and set.

5 – 6   1st couple repeats bars 1 – 2, woman moving from B to C while the man moves from D to A.

7 – 8   1st couple set to each other in new positions.

9 – 10   1st couple repeats bars 1 – 2, woman moving from C to D while the man moves from A to B.

11 – 12   1st couple set to each other in new positions.

13 – 14   1st couple repeats bars 1 – 2, woman moving from D to A while the man moves from B to C.

15 – 16   1st couple set to each other in original positions.

(see over)

17 – 24   1st couple lead down the middle and up again.

25 – 32   1st and 2nd couple poussette.

Repeat, having passed a couple.

Source: introduced by Nathaniel Gow at his Annual Ball, in Edinburgh, 1820. Described in The Ballroom, 1827.

THE REEL OF THE 51ST DIVISION

Bars   **(32 bar reel)**

1 – 8   1st couple set to each other and cast off two places. They meet below 3rd couple and lead up the middle to corners. 2nd couple step up on bars 3 – 4.

9 – 12   1st couple set to and turn first corner with right hands finishing in diagonal line by joining left hands with partner (Fig.).

13 – 14   All balance in line.

15 – 16   1st couple – leaving first corners in place – turn each other one and a quarter times to face second corners.

17 – 22   1st couple repeat bars 9 – 14 with second corners.

23 – 24   1st couple cross to own side one place down.

25 – 32   2nd, 1st and 3rd couples six hands round and back.

Repeat, having passed a couple.

(see over)

Note: when this dance was sent home from Germany, the casting off was given as round three couples. To do this, therefore, would be quite correct, but as the set normally used in Scottish country dances is one of four couples, the Society changed the cast off to the form in which it will be found in the RSCDS books; 'first couple set and cast off two places.'

Source: this dance, planned by Highland Officers, was first performed in a P.O.W. Camp in Germany in presence of Major General Sir Victor M. Fortune, K.B.E., C.B., D.S.O. the Divisional Commander, who granted permission to name it 'The Reel Of The 51st Division' to commemorate the Division in France, 1940.

THE REEL OF THE ROYAL SCOTS

(32 bar reel)

1 – 2   1st and 2nd women turn with left hand, while 1st and 2nd men turn with right hand, 1st couple finishing back to back in the centre of the set in second place.

3 – 4   2nd, 1st and 3rd couples set as in double triangles.

5 – 6   1st and 3rd women turn with right hand, while 1st and 3rd men turn with left hand to change places.

7 – 8   2nd, 3rd and 1st couples set as in double triangles.

9 – 16   1st couple followed by 3rd couple, dance up between the 2nd couple and cast off, then dance down to third place and cast up to second place, 3rd couple finishing in original places. (1st and 3rd couples join nearer hands with partner on every occasion when dancing up or down in the centre) (Fig.).

17 – 24   1st couple turn first corners with right hands,
1st couple pass each other by the right shoulder,
1st couple turn second corners with right hands,
1st couple passing right shoulders cross to second place on own sides.

(see over)

25 – 32 2nd, 1st and 3rd couples six hands round and back.

Repeat having passed a couple.

Source: devised by Roy Goldring to celebrate the 350th Anniversary of The Royal Scots (The Royal Regiment) in 1983.

REEL OF TULLOCH

This is danced to its own tune and to no other. It may also follow a strathspey and reel, or a strathspey only, when the time changes immediately after the final setting.

Bars   *(Reel)*

Reel Of Tulloch only.
Partners stand side by side as in 'Foursome Reel' (Fig. 1).

TOP

1

1 – 8   Women enter the centre and set (Fig. 2).

2

9 – 16   Women turn (see note) left and finish facing the opposite man (Fig. 3 overleaf).

17 – 24   All set.

(see over)

3

25 – 32   All turn, finishing men in centre (Fig. 4).

4

33 – 64   Repeat as above. Men set and turn. All set and turn, finishing with women in centre.

65 – 128   Repeat bars 1 – 64 as above and at the end of the dance finish beside partners (Fig. 1).

    Reel of Tulloch following Strathspey or Strathspey and Reel

    Begins after setting steps.

1 – 8   Women dancing in set, while men dance out.

    Continue as 'Reel of Tulloch'.

164

Note

1. *When turning in this dance, right arms are linked for four bars, then left arms. The figure below shows the arm positions when two women turn. When two men turn, or a man and a woman turn, it is normal to use elbow grip.*

2. *At a conference where Highland, ballroom, military and country dancers and pipers were represented, it was agreed that an effort should be made to standardise the Foursome Reel. The following suggestions were made:-*
   1. *When danced as a dance by itself, it should take the form of*
      4 Strathspey and
      4 Reel or Reel of Tulloch.
   2. *When a Foursome Reel follows immediately after an Eightsome, it should take a shorter form, i.e. 2 Strathspey and 2 Reel or Half Reel of Tulloch (1–64) with women finishing beside their partners on the opposite side of the dance.*

Source: unknown, but believed to have been first danced on a very cold morning by parishioners standing outside of the kirk at Tulloch waiting for the doors to open; to keep warm, they turned each other and so developed the dance.

ROUND REEL OF EIGHT

Eightsome Reel formation

Bars   *(Reel)*

1 – 8   All 4 women cast by the right and dance outside the set back to original places.

9 – 16   All 4 men repeat bars 1 – 8 but cast by the left.

17 – 32   Grand chain half-way round in six steps. All set to partners, continue grand chain back to original places in six steps and set to partners.

33 – 35   1st and 3rd couples change places. 1st couple dance between 3rd couple (Fig. 1)

1

36 – 38   Repeat bars 33 – 35 back to original places. 3rd couple dance between 1st couple.

39 – 40   1st and 3rd couples turn with right hands into allemande hold ready for promenade.

41 – 48   1st and 3rd couples promenade round the inside of the set back to original places (Fig. 2).

2

49 – 64 2nd and 4th couples repeat bars 33 – 48. 2nd couple dance between 4th couple on bars 49 – 51; 4th couple between 2nd couple on bars 52 – 54.

65 – 68 1st and 3rd couple dance half rights and lefts.

69 – 72 2nd and 4th couples dance half rights and lefts.

73 – 80 Repeat bars 65 – 72 back to original places.

81 – 88 All 4 couples dance eight hands round and back.

Source: Thompson, 1751.

THE SAILOR

Bars *(32 bar reel)*

1 – 2   1st couple, giving right hands, cross over, 1st woman to face 2nd and 3rd men, 1st man to face 2nd and 3rd woman. 2nd couple step up.

3 – 4   Joining nearer hands, they set in threes on the sides of the dance (Fig.).

5 – 8   1st woman casts up round 2nd man to stand between 2nd couple, all facing down, while 1st man casts down round 3rd woman to stand between 3rd couple, all facing up. Joining nearer hands, all set.

9 – 16   Reels of 3 across the dance. 1st couple, turning to the right, giving right shoulder to begin the reel, and finish in 2nd place on the opposite side of the dance.

17 – 24 1st couple lead down the middle (two steps) and up, crossing at the top to cast into second place on own sides.

25 – 32 2nd and 1st couples dance rights and lefts.

Repeat, having passed a couple.

Source: collected by Jenny MacLachlan

SCOTTISH REFORM

Bars   *(32 bar jig)*

1 – 2   1st couple turn with right hands to position as in Fig. 1.

1

3 – 4   1st and 2nd couples balance in line.

5 – 6   1st man and 2nd woman, 1st woman and 2nd man turn with left hands to position as in Fig. 2.

2

7 – 8   1st and 2nd couples balance in line.

9 – 10   1st man and 2nd woman, 1st woman and 2nd man turn with left hands to position as in Fig. 1.

(see over)

11 – 12   1st and 2nd couples balance in line.

13 – 16   1st couple turn with right hands to original positions. (1st couple, using four skip change of step, dance across into own places at the top and round, turning by the right to meet, ready to go down the middle.)

17 – 24   1st couple lead down the middle and up again.

25 – 32   1st and 2nd couples poussette.

Repeat, having passed a couple.

Note: this dance is called 'The Prince of Wales' in Lochaber and Mull and danced to the tune 'Kenmure's on and awa' ', with the words am faicinn thu tighinn mo bhalachan bhan...till mo righ mo bhalachan bhan, *etc. (Do I see you coming, my fair-haired lad? My King returns, my fair-haired lad).*

Source: collected in Perthshire and Argyll.

SIXTEENSOME (OR DOUBLE EIGHTSOME) REEL

This is a square dance taken part in by eight couples. Each side of the square is formed of two couples of which the right hand couple (odd numbers) are called 'inside' and left hand couples (even numbers) are called 'outside'.

Bars   *(Reel)*

(A)

1 – 4   All join hands and slip round to the left for eight steps (Fig. 1).

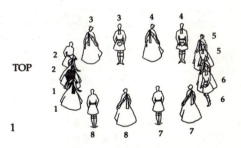

5 – 8   Still holding hands, dance round in the opposite direction eight slip steps. This brings everyone back to their original places.

9 – 16   All men retain their partners' left hand in their right. The inside women, 1, 3, 5 and 7, give right hands across, and the outside women give their right hands to the inside men (Fig. 2 overleaf).

(see over)

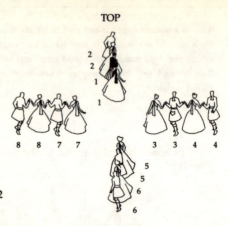

They all dance right round and finish in a double circle (Fig. 3).

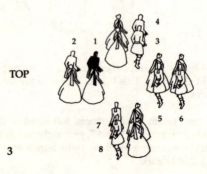

17 – 20   All set to partners twice.

172

21 – 24   All turn partners with both hands.

25 – 40   Grand Chain.
    The inside couples, 1, 3, 5 and 7, form a small chain in the centre while the outside couples 2, 4, 6 and 8, form a chain outside the first chain. End in places as in Fig. 1.
    Inside couples (1, 3, 5 and 7) use pas de basque while outside couples (2, 4, 6 and 8) use skip change of step.

(B)
    Two 'inside' women (1 and 5) now go into the centre of the dance and set to one another 4 bars, turn each other 4 bars, as in 'Reel of Tulloch', while the other 14 all take hands and dance round them.

1 – 4   Eight slip steps to the left.

5 – 8   Eight slip steps back to places.

9 – 12   1st and 5th women set to and turn partners.

13 – 16   1st woman sets to and turns 6th man while 5th woman sets to and turns 2nd man.

17 – 24   Reels of three – 1st woman with 6th and 1st men, and 5th woman with 2nd and 5th men. 1st and 5th women stay in centre as before (setting and turning one another). The others dance round them.

25 – 28   Eight slip steps to the left.

29 – 32   Eight slip steps back to places.

33 – 36   1st woman sets to and turns man at her nearest corner, i.e. 8th man. 5th woman sets to and turns man at her nearest corner, i.e 4th man
    (see over)

37 – 40 1st woman sets to and turns 3rd man. 5th woman sets to and turns 7th man.

41 – 48 Reels of three –
1st woman with 3rd and 8th men.
5th woman with 7th and 4th men.
The 1st and 5th women retire to their places and the 2nd and 6th women go into the centre.

Repeat all (B)

The 'outside' women 2nd and 6th are now in the centre. For bars 9 – 16 they set first to their partners and then 2nd woman sets to 5th man while 6th woman sets to 1st man.

On bars 33 – 40 they set to and turn their nearest corners, i.e. 2nd woman sets to 3rd man then 8th man, while 6th women sets to 7th man then 4th man.

When all women have had their turn in the centre of the dance, the men each have their turn beginning with numbers 1 and 5, each man dancing with the women in the same manner as described in B.

When all eight men have had their turn, repeat all (A).

Note: when odd numbers are in the centre they set to one another for 4 bars, then swing with right arms (as in Reel of Tulloch) for 4 bars. The second time they are in the centre they swing with left arms. When even numbers are in the centre they swing first with left arms, second time with right arms.

STRIP THE WILLOW
(DROPS OF BRANDY)

Bars (9/8 jig)

1 – 4 1st couple turn with right hands, two and a half times. (12 running steps).

5 – 6 1st woman and 2nd man turn with left hands, while 1st man runs down the middle to meet his partner. 6 running steps (Fig. 1).

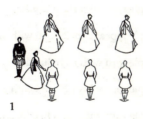

1

7 – 8 1st couple turn with right hands. 6 running steps.

9 – 12 Repeat bars 5 – 8 but 1st woman turns 3rd man.

13 – 16 Repeat bars 5 – 8 but 1st woman turns 4th man.

17 – 28 1st couple repeat bars 5 – 16 travelling up the woman's side of the dance, i.e. 1st man turns 4th woman with left hand then partner with right hand; 3rd woman with left hand then partner with right hand; 2nd woman with left hand then partner with right hand.

29 – 30 1st woman and 2nd man turn with left hands while 1st man and 2nd woman turn with left hands (Fig. 2 overleaf).

(see over)

2

31 – 32   1st couple turn with right hands.

33 – 34   1st couple repeat bars 29 – 30 with 3rd couple.

35 – 36   1st couple turn with right hands.

37 – 38   1st couple repeat bars 29 – 30 with 4th couple.

39 – 40   1st couple turn with right hands, one and a half times. (See note 4 below)

Repeat with new top couple. (See note 4)

Note:
1. *Running step (see p.42) is used throughout this dance, 3 steps to each bar.*
2. *The set remains in the same place by the moving up of each couple as they are turned by the 1st couple during bars 29 – 38.*
3. *The numbering of the bars is for a four couple set.*
4. *A new top couple begins at the end of each 40 bars of music, which means the couple finishing their turn of the dance must use the 1st two bars of music for the new top couple. 4th couple would therefore only be able to turn each other to own sides at the completion of their turn of the dance.*
Source: collected locally

THE TRIUMPH

Bars   *(24 bar reel)*

1 – 8   1st man leads 1st woman down the middle and up again,
            then passing his partner in front of him presents her to 2nd
            man.

9 – 12   2nd man and 1st woman dance down the middle with
            nearer hands joined, 1st man following (Fig. 1).

1

The woman now turns round by the right, retaining the 2nd
man's left hand in her right hand. She crosses her arms,
giving her left hand to her partner. The 1st man with his left
hand takes the 2nd man's right hand, and raising them as
high as possible behind the 1st woman's head (Fig. 2).

2

(see over)

13 – 16   1st woman with 1st and 2nd men dance up the middle in triumph. 2nd man breaks off and returns to his own place.

17 – 24   1st couple poussette to the bottom of the dance, where they stand. 2nd, 3rd and 4th couples step up on bars 23 – 24.

Repeat with a new top couple.

Note:
This poussette is done as follows: –
1. *1st man is still on opposite side of dance; quarter turn (man pulls all the time with right hand);*
2. *progress down the dance;*
3. *quarter turn;*
4. *quarter turn;*
5. *progress;*
6. *progress and be turning;*
7. *turn to own side of dance;*
8. *fall back to sides.*

Source: collected locally; also described in The Ballroom, *1827.*
Introduced by Nathaniel Gow 1808.

WALTZ COUNTRY DANCE

Stand in groups of four round the room, one couple facing another, women on the right-hand side of their partners.

Bars   *(40 bar waltz)*

1 – 4   Each man and woman sets to the man and woman opposite then crosses to change places, passing right shoulder, women making a waltz turn by the right while men moving straight forward.

5 – 8   Set to partners and change places as in bars 3 – 4.

9 – 16   Repeat bars 1 – 8 and finish in original starting positions.

17 – 18   All four joining hands, balance forward and backward.

19 – 20   Men balancing on the spot bring the women on their left over to the place on their right (with both hands) (Fig. 1).

1

21 – 32   Repeat bars 17 – 20, three more times.

33 – 40   Poussette, passing couple with whom they have just danced to meet the next couple. To begin this poussette, the men push their partners backwards – those going clockwise into

(see over)

the centre of the circle and the other couple away from the centre of the circle (Fig. 2).

2

Repeat with next couple.

Note: a slow pas de basque is used in this dance.

Source: described in The Ballroom, 1827 *as 'The Guaracha', a Spanish dance.*

WAVERLEY
(FERGUS MCIVER)

Bars

(48 bar jig)

1 – 8   With 1st woman leading, 1st, 2nd and 3rd women dance round 1st, 2nd and 3rd men (Fig. 1).

1

9 – 16   1st, 2nd and 3rd men dance round the three women.

17 – 24   1st couple facing down, 2nd couple facing up, set, and giving right hands in passing, change places with person opposite. Repeat back to own places, giving left hands in passing.

25 – 32   1st and 2nd couples poussette. 1st couple finish back to back in the middle facing own sides of dance (Fig. *2*).

2   15z

(see over)

33 – 40   Double Triangles. 1st couple finish facing the woman's side of dance.
1st man after making triangles with 2nd and 3rd woman, must do a full turn right about to join right hands with his partner, facing the women's side of the dance ready to lead through. 1st woman does a half turn to her right to get into the position.

41 – 48   1st couple lead through between 2nd and 3rd women, 1st woman casts up and 1st man casts down. They meet in the middle of the dance, cast as before, between 2nd and 3rd men, and finish on own sides of dance one place down (Fig. 3).

3

Repeat having passed a couple.

Source: Button and Whitaker. 1812.

WEST'S HORNPIPE

Bars

(32 bar reel)

1 – 8 1st woman dances a reel of three with 2nd and 3rd men finishing in her partner's place while 1st man does same with 2nd and 3rd women (Fig. 1).

1

9 – 16 1st, 2nd and 3rd couples dance reels of three on own sides.

17 – 24 1st couple lead down the middle and up again turning inwards on last step to face 2nd couple diagonally (Fig. 2).

2

25 – 28 1st couple set to 2nd couple and, joining nearer hands, dance to fourth place and turn inwards. 2nd, 3rd and 4th couples step up on bars 27 – 28.

29 – 32 4th and 1st couples dance four hands round.

Repeat with new couple.

Source: The Ladies' Pocket Book, *1797.*

THE WHITE COCKADE

Bars

1 – 8   1st, 2nd and 3rd couples set and cross over giving right hands, then set and cross back to original places, again giving right hands.

9 – 16   1st couple lead down the middle and up again to top place in the middle of the dance.

17 – 20   1st couple cast off to second place on own sides (Fig.).

2nd couple step up on bars 19 – 20.

21 – 24   1st and 3rd couples dance four hands round to the left.

25 – 32   2nd and 1st couples dance rights and lefts.

Repeat, having passed a couple.

Source: Preston, 24 New Country Dances for the year 1797.

THE WILD GEESE

Bars   *(32 bar jig)*

1 – 4   1st and 3rd couples advance into the middle (2 pas de
              basque), men with their partners on their right. All join
              hands to make a line of four, and set (Fig. 1).

1

5 – 8   1st couple dance a three-quarter turn with right hands to
              cast off to 3rd place on their own sides of the dance.
              Meanwhile, 3rd couple turn each other with right hand to
              face up the middle on their own sides and lead up to top
              place.

9 – 16   3rd and 1st couples repeat bars 1 – 8, but 1st couple now do
              the movement as danced by 3rd couple, and 3rd couple the
              movement as danced by 1st couple (Fig. 2). All finish in
              original places.

2

(see over)

17 – 24   1st couple lead down the middle and up, to finish in second place. 2nd couple step up on bars 19 – 20.

25 – 32   2nd and 1st couples dance rights and lefts.

Repeat, having passed a couple.

Source: collected by Jenny MacLachlan.

Country Dances
from
Other Sources

THE BEES OF MAGGIEKNOCKATER

Bars   *(32 bar jig for 4 couples)*

1 – 4   1st couple, giving right hands in passing, cross over to opposite sides and cast off to second place (2nd couple step up on bars 3 – 4).

5 – 8   1st and 3rd couples dance right hands across.
At the end:
3rd woman turns towards 1st man, retaining hold of his right hand, then joins left hands with him in promenade hold facing out towards the woman's side; 1st woman dances similarly with 3rd man so that they finish facing out towards the men's side of the dance.

9 – 12   Reels of three on the sides. 1st man and 3rd woman, dancing together, dance half a reel of three on the women's side with 4th and 2nd women. They pass 4th woman by the right to begin, 1st woman and 3rd man, dancing together, similarly dance half a reel of three on the men's side with 2nd and 4th men. They pass 2nd man by the right to begin. On bar 12, when they meet in the middle of the dance, 1st and 3rd couples drop hands and join hands with partners in promenade hold so that 1st couple are facing towards the men's side and 3rd couple facing towards the women's side.

Bar 9

13 – 16   Continuing the reels of three on the sides:
1st couple dance half a reel of three on the men's side with 2nd and 4th men, passing 2nd man (in fourth place) by the left; 3rd couple dance half a reel of three on the women's side with 4th and 2nd women, passing 4th lady (in top place) by the left. On bar 16 1st man and 3rd woman join hands in promenade hold facing the men's side, while 1st woman and 3rd man join hands in promenade hold facing the women's side.

Bar 13

17 – 20   Continuing the reels of three on the sides:
1st man and 3rd woman dance on the men's side passing 2nd man by the right. 1st lady and 3rd man dance on the women's side passing 4th lady by the right. On bar 20 1st and 3rd couples join hands with partners.

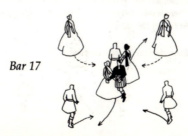

Bar 17

(see over)

21 – 24 Continuing the reels of three on the sides:-
1st couple dance on the women's side passing 4th woman
by the left. 3rd couple dance on the men's side passing 2nd
man by the left.

Bar 21

25 – 28 1st man turns 3rd woman with the left hand one and a half
times to leave her in second place; 1st woman, similarly,
turns 3rd man with the right hand. At the end 1st couple
dance down crossing over to face 4th couple on own sides.

29 – 32 1st man turns 4th man one and a half times with the right
hand; 1st woman turns 4th woman with the left hand. 1st
couple finish in fourth place.

Repeat with a new top couple.

*Note: Maggieknockater is a hamlet two miles north-east of Craigellachie.
In a field there beside the road was a large sign - 'Maggieknockater Apiary'
- hence the title of this dance.*

Source: dance devised by John Drewry.

THE BELLE OF BON ACCORD

Bars   *(32 bar strathspey for 4 couples)*

1 – 4   1st woman dances down between 2nd couple crossing over to the men's side, she casts up behind 2nd man, then dances into the middle to face down. 1st man dances straight across the dance passing his partner by the right, he casts off behind 2nd woman, then dances into the middle to face up. 3rd couple dance similarly round 4th couple. (2nd and 4th couples should move up very slightly between bars 3 – 4 certainly not a whole place). See Fig.

5 – 8   1st couple with 2nd couple, and 3rd couple with 4th couple, dance right hands across. 1st and 3rd couples finish in a straight line down the middle of the dance, with the ladies facing down and the men facing up.

9 – 16   1st and 3rd couples dance a reel of four down the middle of the dance, finishing the reel in the places from which they began it.

17 – 18   1st couple turn by the right hand to finish in second place facing up with nearer hands joined. (1st woman is on her partners left). 2nd couple dance up on the sides, then in, to join nearer hands facing down. 3rd and 4th couples dance similarly.

(see over)

19 – 24   1st couple set to 2nd couple then dance four hands round to the left. 3rd and 4th couples dance similarly. All finish to the side lines in the order 2, 1, 4, 3 with 1st and 3rd couples on opposite sides.

25 – 28   1st couple, joining right hands, lead up between 2nd couple crossing to own sides and cast off to second place, while 3rd couple dance similarly round 4th couple.

29 – 30   1st and 3rd couples turn partners with both hands opening up to face down.

31 – 32   1st couple dance down to 4th place, while 3rd couple cast up to second place.

Repeat with a new top couple.

Source: dance devised by John Drewry.

BLOOMS OF BON ACCORD

2 chords. On the second chord, 3rd and 4th couples cross
over to opposite sides

Bars   *(32 bar reel for 4 couples)*

1 – 8   1st and 2nd couples, joining nearer hands, set on the sides,
dance right hands across once round, then 1st couple cast
off to second place while second couple dance up to top
place. 3rd and 4th couple dance similarly. On bars 7– 8, 4th
couple cast up to third place, while 3rd couple dance down
to fourth place. (They are still on opposite sides.)

9 – 12   1st couple giving right hands, cross the dance, cast up on
opposite sides behind 2nd couple, then dance in to join
hands in promenade hold facing down. 4th couple, similarly, cross the dance, cast off on own sides behind 3rd couple,
then dance in to join hands in promenade hold facing up.

13 – 16   1st and 4th couples dance round one another, the ladies
passing right shoulders, so that 1st couple finish in the
middle of the men's side facing up, while 4th couple finish
in the middle of the women's side facing down (Fig. 1).

17 – 24   1st couple, dancing together, dance a reel of three on the
men's side with 2nd man and 3rd woman. 1st couple pass
2nd man by the right to begin, and finish in the middle of
the dance in third place facing up.

(see over)

4th couple, similarly, dance a reel of three on the women's side with 3rd man and 2nd woman. 4th couple pass 3rd man by the right to begin, and finish in the centre of the dance in second place facing down (Fig 2).

2

25 – 28   Dropping left hands, 1st and 4th couples dance right hands across once round. At the end, 1st and 4th men retain hold of their partners by the right hand and turn towards them, so that 4th couple finish in second place facing up, while 1st couple finish in third place facing down.

29 – 32   4th couple lead up between 2nd couple, crossing over to own sides, and cast off the second place, while 1st couple lead down between 3rd couple, crossing over to opposite sides, and cast up to third place.

The finishing order in 2, 4, 1, 3 with 1st and 3rd couples on opposite sides.

Repeat with a new top couple.

Note: this dance was devised in 1971 to commemorate the winning by the City of Aberdeen of the 'Britain in Bloom' competition for the third successive year.

Source: dance devised by John Drewry.

THE CELTIC CROSS

Bars   *(4 x 48 bar reel in a square set)*

1 – 4   All four women dance right hands across once round; at the same time the men dance anti-clockwise half-way round the outside (Fig. 1).

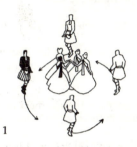

1

5 – 8   Retaining right hands, women give left hands to the opposite man, (1st woman and 3rd man, 2nd woman and 4th man, 3rd woman and 1st man, 4th woman and 2nd man). All set, then half-turn, left hands, to bring the men to the centre, women to the outside.

9 – 12   Men dance right hands across once round while the women dance anti-clockwise half-way round the outside (Fig. 2).

2

(see over)

13 – 16 Retaining right hands, the men give left hands to partners. All set then quarter turn, left hands, onto the side opposite original places.

17 – 24 1st and 3rd couples advance (2 steps), retire (2 steps); then dance half rights and lefts.

25 – 32 2nd and 4th couples repeat bars 17 – 24.

33 – 40 All set to partners and turn them right hand; set to corners then turn them three quarters, right hand, into promenade hold.

41 – 48 Men promenade their corners once round anti-clockwise. Men finish in their original places with their new partner.

On last bar, men bring new partners across in front of them ready to repeat.

Source: dance devised by Derek Haynes.

CURLYWEE

(32 bar strathspey)

1 – 4   1st and 2nd men (and women likewise), taking nearer hands, set, approaching. On the second step 1st man dances across in front of 2nd man, to finish on his right hand side facing up; women dance likewise finishing facing down. Taking nearer hands, all set (Fig. 1).

1

5 – 8   All set, and on the second step 2nd man dances across in front of 1st man to finish on his right hand side facing across; women dance likewise. Taking nearer hands, all set, retiring to the sidelines (on the opposite side).

9 – 12   1st couple lead up, crossing to own sides, and cast off round 2nd couple.

13 – 16   2nd couple lead down, crossing to own sides, and cast up round 1st couple.

17 – 20   1st and 2nd couples, cross, giving right hands (Fig. 2 overleaf), form a circle and dance four hands half round to the left.

21 – 24   They cross again, giving left hands (Fig. 3 overleaf), form a circle and dance four hands half round to the right.

(see over)

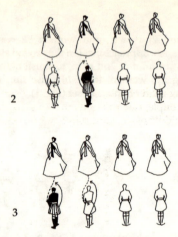

25 – 32   Double figure of eight (Fig. 4): 1st couple begin by leading up, crossing to opposite sides; 2nd couple begin by casting off. All end the figure of eight where they started it. Repeat, having passed a couple.

Source: devised by Hugh Foss.
Reproduced by permission of Scottish National Dance Company, Reading

THE DUKE AND DUCHESS OF EDINBURGH

Bars   *(40 bar reel)*

1 – 8 1st, 2nd and 3rd couples, with hands joined, advance and retire then all turn own partners and return to places.

9 – 16 1st couple cast off one place on own sides, lead down between 3rd couple, cast up round them, lead up between 2nd couple, cast round them into second place finishing in the middle of set. (2nd couple move up) (Fig. 1).

1

17 – 20 1st woman dances three hands across (right hands) with the second couple while 1st man does the same with the 3rd couple (Fig. 2), passing right shoulders at the finish.

2

21 – 24 Three hands across, (left hands) the first woman with the 3rd couple and 1st man with 2nd couple (Fig. 3, overleaf), finishing by passing left shoulders to face first corners.

(see over)

3

25 – 32   1st couple turn first corners with right hands, then partners with left hands; turn second corners with right hands, and giving left hands in passing cross over to own sides of dance, one place down.

33–40   1st, 2nd and 3rd couples dance six hands round and back.

Repeat, having passed a couple.

Note:
1. *On bars 5 – 8, all turn partners with both hands but with skip change of step. This is the 'Edinburgh Style' of turning with both hands. At the end, 1st couple stay facing out*
2. *On bars 7 – 8, in some areas it is customary for 1st woman to finish facing the top with nearer hand joined with partner before dancing out to place.*
3. *On bars 9 – 16, 1st couple have a long way to travel and so must dance without hesitation. They join nearer hands where possible and pass left shoulders on bar 16.*

Source: dance devised by Allie Anderson and Florence Leslie.

Reproduced by permission of Rae Macintosh (Music) Ltd/ Music Sales Ltd, London.

THE DUNEDIN FESTIVAL DANCE

Dancers are in circles of three couples, with women on their partner's right.

Bars   *(32 bar hornpipe)*

1 – 8   All dance six hands round and back (Fig.).

9 – 12   All face partners and dance back to back with them.

13 – 16   All turn partners giving right hands.

17 – 20   All dance right hands across (i.e. six hands) in a wheel.

21 – 24   The man with his hand underneath pulls the woman oppo-
          site (his new partner) under the hands of the others and
          they take promenade hold. The next man does the same,
          and the 3rd man pulls his new partner towards him. All
          keep dancing in a circular movement for all eight bars.

25 – 30   All promenade at random about the room.

31 – 32   Each couple joins up with another two couples to make a
          circle.

          Repeat ad lib.

(see over)

Note: dance adapted from Derek Haynes' 'Borrowdale Exchange' and presented to Dunedin Dancers. It was first used as a mixing dance for the 11th Dunedin International Folk Dance Festival, held in 1991.

Reprinted by kind permission of the Dunedin Dancers.

DUNNET HEAD

(32 bar reel for 4 couples)

1 – 8 1st woman, followed by 2nd, 3rd and 4th women dances across the top of the set, down behind the men, across the bottom of the set, and up own side to place.

9 – 16 1st man, followed by 2nd, 3rd and 4th men, dances across the top of the set, down behind the women, across the bottom of the set, and up own side to place.

17 – 24 All dance eight hands round and back.

25 – 28 All four women, and all four men, taking hands on the side, advance for two steps and retire for two steps.

29 – 32 1st couple dance down to fourth place, 2nd, 3rd and 4th couples step up.

Note: Dunnet Head is the most northerly point on the British mainland. Source: dance devised by Peter Knight.

THE FOURSOME REEL

There are different versions of the Foursome Reel. Before 1940, it was frequently known as the Scotch Reel & Reel of Tulloch. In the army in the 1940s, it was usually danced having four strathspey steps followed by a half Reel of Tulloch. The Foursome Reel is still danced today in some parts of Scotland, as it has been danced since the earlier part of this century, having three strathspey steps, followed by eight bars of Reel time, which may be danced in one of the following three ways.

A. Women dance round to their left in a circle for eight steps, returning to their place, the men follow their opposite partner whom they are facing, in the chase. The men finish back to back facing their own partner.

B. Men join their left hand with the right hand of their opposite partner, moving into a circle. All four dance four hands twice round to the left women returning to their own place while the men finish back to back facing their own partner.

C. Sometimes the four dancers from a basket dancing round to their left, although this is undesirable in a crowded ballroom.

Following the chase, circle or basket, all begin the Reel of Tulloch by setting to their own partner followed by a Tulloch swing. With the women now in the centre, the half Reel of Tulloch can begin; that is. four more times. Note: the music required for this version is three strathspey and five and a half times the Reel of Tulloch.

Strathspey Setting Steps (A)
(Lord James Stewart Murray's Setting Step)

Bars	Counting	Description of Step
1	One	A: Hop on the left foot and extend the right foot to Second position
	Two	B: Hop on the left foot and place the right foot behind the calf of the left leg

Bars	Counting	Description of Step	
	Three	C:	Hop on the left foot and extend the right foot to Fourth position
	Four	D:	Hop on the left foot and place the right foot in front of the left leg, just below the knee
2		A – D:	Repeat bar 1 (A to D) above beginning with the left foot and hopping on the right foot
3		A – D:	Repeat bar 1 (A to D) above beginning with the right foot and hopping on the left foot
4		E:	Four spring points to Fourth position beginning with the left foot: i.e. left, right, left, right
5 – 8		A – E:	Repeat bars 1 – 4 (A to E) beginning with the left foot

Arms: alternate arms raised must be opposite to the working foot. Both arms raised for spring points.

To recap above:
Right foot: side, behind, point and lift
Left foot: repeat above
Right foot: repeat above
Finishing with four spring points: left, right, left, right

Repeat whole step beginning with the left foot

Strathspey Setting Steps (B)
(Huntly or Change Step)

Bars	Counting	Description of Step
1	One	A: Hop on the left foot & extend the right foot to Second position

Bars	Counting		Description of Step
	Two	B:	Hop on the left foot & place the right foot behind the calf of the left leg
	Three	C:	Hop on the left foot & place the right foot in front of the left leg just below the knee
	Four	D:	Hop on the left foot & place the right foot behind the calf of the left leg
2	One	E:	Hop on the left foot & extend the right foot to Second position
	Two	F:	Hop on the left foot & place the right foot behind the calf of the left leg
	Three	G:	Hop on to the right foot & place the left foot behind the calf of the right leg
	Four	H:	Hop on the right foot placing the left foot into Third position in front of the right leg
3 – 4		A – H:	Repeat bars 1–2 (A to H) above beginning with the left foot & hopping on the right foot
5 – 8			Repeat bars 1–4 beginning with the right foot once more

Arms: alternate arms raised must be opposite to the working foot.

To recap above:
Right foot: side, behind, in front, behind
Right foot: side, behind, change, down

Repeat step beginning with the left foot

Reel Setting Steps (A)
(Pas de basque & points)
This step is suitable for both men & women

Bars	Counting	Description of Step	
1		A:	One pas de basque on to right foot finishing with the left foot extended forward to Fourth position
			Two spring points:
2	One/&	B:	Hop on to left foot (replacing right foot) & extending the right foot to Fourth position
	Two/&	C:	Hop on to right foot (replacing left foot) & extending the left foot to Fourth position
3 – 4		A – C:	Repeat bars 1–2 (A to C) again beginning with a pas de basque on to left foot
5 – 6		D:	Two pas de basque, right foot & left foot; finish with the right foot extended to Fourth position
7 – 8		E:	Four spring points to Fourth position beginning with the left foot: i.e. left, right, left, right

Arms: down for the pas de basque. Both arms are raised for spring points.

To recap above:
Pas de basque right, point right & left
Pas de basque left, point left & right
Pas de basque right, pas de basque left
Points: left, right, left, right

Reel Setting Steps (B)
(Balance or coupe & pas de basque)
This step is suitable for both women and men

Stand with the right foot extended forward to Fourth Intermediate position – raised

Bars	Counting	Description of Step
1		Balance Step:
	One/&	A: Hop on to right foot bringing it down in place of the left which is extended to Fourth intermediate position, rear raised
	Two/&	B: Hop on to left foot bringing it down in place of the right which is extended forward once more to Fourth Intermediate position raised
2		C: Pas de basque on to right foot finishing with the left foot extended forward to Fourth Intermediate position raised
3–4		A–C: Repeat bars 1–2 (A to C) beginning with the left foot, and finishing with the right foot extended forward to Fourth Intermediate position raised
5–8		Repeat bars 1–4 beginning with the right foot once more

Arms: both arms are raised for the balance step. Down for the pas de basque

To recap above:
Balance, balance pas de basque right
Balance, balance pas de basque left
Balance, balance pas de basque right
Balance, balance Pas de Basque left

This step may also be danced beginning with pas de basque and then balance. This version is used in 'Lord MacLay's Reel'.

The Foursome Reel
(Traditional Version)

The Foursome Reel is danced by 2 couples facing each other across the room. The men have their partners on their right as in Fig. 1.

TOP

1

Bars   *(48 bar strathspey / 88 bar reel)*

Strathspey

1 – 8   Both couples dance a reel of four across the room (Fig. 2), finishing as in Fig. 3.
Note: in starting the dance, men stand for two bars while the women pass left shoulder in the centre.

2   3

(see over)

209

Bars

9 – 16   All set with Highland setting step.

17 – 24   Repeat the reel of four, finishing as in Fig. 4.
          Note: pass right shoulder with the person you are facing to
          begin the reel of four.

25 – 32   All set with Highland setting steps.

33 – 40   Repeat the reel of four, finishing as in Fig. 3 (overleaf).

40 – 48   All set with Highland setting steps.

Reel of Tulloch

1 – 8   All dance round to the left, by one of the ways described
          above, A, B, or C. Finish as in Fig. 4.

9 – 16   All set to partner with Highland setting steps.

17 – 24   All tulloch turn own partner by one of the methods
          described below. Women are now facing each other in the
          centre (Fig. 5 above).

25 – 32   Women set to each other.

33 – 40   Women tulloch turn so they now face opposite partner (Fig. 6).

41 – 48 All set to opposite partner.

49 – 56 All tulloch turn opposite partner, men now face each other in the centre (Fig. 7).

57 – 64 Men set to each other.

65 – 72 Men tulloch turn so they now face own partner (Fig. 8).

73 – 80 All set to partner.

81 – 88 All tulloch turn, finishing beside partner, facing the other couple, but on the opposite side of the set from where they started the strathspey.

When turning in the reel of tulloch, arms are linked as shown below for 4 bars, then change direction linked the other way for 4 bars. It is customary for men and men and women to use the elbow grip; women may also find this easier (Fig. 9).

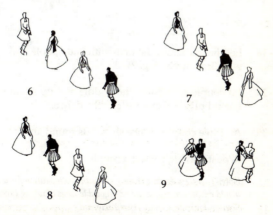

Source: collected by W. Clement

211

GOOD HEARTED GLASGOW

Bars   *(32 bar jig)*

1 – 4   1st couple turn each other with right hands and cast off one place on own side. 2nd couple move up.

5 – 8   1st couple turn each other with left hands one and a quarter times ready for -

9 – 12   Right hands across, 1st man with 3rd couple and 1st woman with 2nd couple (Fig. 1). All finish on the side lines.

1

2

13 – 16   Left hands across, 1st man with 2nd couple and 1st woman with 3rd couple (Fig. 2).

17 – 24   1st couple lead down the middle and up again to finish in second place on own side of the dance.

25 – 32   All three couples dance six hands round and back again.

Repeat, having passed a couple.

Note: This jig was the winning entry in a competition for a dance which would encourage people to find enjoyable ways of taking exercise.
Source: dance devised by Peter Knapman.
Reproduced by kind permission of Glasgow Branch, RSCDS.

THE HIGHLANDMAN'S UMBRELLA

Bars   *(Reel for 4 couples / square set)*

1 – 4   All four couples taking promenade hold advance and retire (Fig.).

5 – 8   The four women casting by the right dance round one place clockwise.

9 – 12   All four couples taking promenade hold with new partner advance and retire.

13 – 16 The four men casting by the left dance round one place counterclockwise.

17 – 18 All set to new partner.

19 – 20 1st and 3rd men change places giving left hand.

21 – 22 2nd and 4th men change places giving left hand.

23 – 24 All set to original partner.

25 – 32 Eight hands round and back.

(see over)

Repeat from new position.

Note: each couple has progressed one place clockwise at the end of each 32 bars. The men who cross first with left hand (bars 19 – 20) are on the sides of the set each time.

Source: dance devised by Anna Holden of Birmingham Branch, RSCDS.

Reproduced by kind permission of Glasgow Branch, RSCDS.

THE HIGHLAND RAMBLER

Bars *(40 bar reel for 3 couples)*

1 – 4   1st couple dance in towards each other and cast off one place. 2nd couple step up on bars 3 – 4

5 – 8   1st and 3rd couples dance right hands across. Note: at the end of bar 8, 1st woman does not make a turn before beginning the left hands across.

9 – 12   2nd and 1st couples dance left hands across; 1st couple finish facing women's side of the dance.

13 – 16   1st woman, followed by her partner, casts up round the 2nd woman and dances down the middle to finish between 3rd couple; 1st man finishes between 2nd couple (Fig.). All face down.

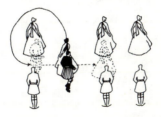

17 – 24   All dance down the middle and, turning right about, all dance up. 1st couple remain facing up on bar 24.

25 – 28   1st man, followed by his partner, casts off to second place on the women's side and crosses to his own side. On bar 28, he pulls back his right shoulder to face his partner.

29 – 32   1st couple turn with right hands once round, to finish in second place on own sides.

(see over)

33 – 40   2nd, 1st and 3rd couples dance six hands round and back.

Repeat having passed a couple.

Source: dance devised by Roy Goldring.
Reproduced by kind permission of the Leeds Branch, RSCDS

A HIGHLAND WELCOME

The dancers stand in fours, all round the room, each man having his partner on his right side, and another couple opposite, everyone dancing at the same time (see Fig.).

Bars   *(32 bar reel)*

1 – 8   Both couples with slip steps circle to left for 4 bars and back to the right for 4 bars.

9 – 16   Both couples now dance right hands across for 4 steps (skip change of step), then giving left hands across, back to place.

17 – 20   Now give left hand to the person opposite and turn once round to finish facing partner.

21 – 24   Give right hand to partner and turn once round to finish facing the other couple with whom you have been dancing.

25 – 28   Join inside hands with partner, all advance for two steps and retire for two steps (skip change of step).

29 – 32   Couples facing clockwise round the room make an arch.

(see over)

All advance for four steps with the couples facing anti-clockwise passing under the arch made by the other couple, to meet a new couple.

Repeat with new couples as often as desired.

Source: devised by Bill Forbes.

LETHAM LADIES

Bars

(40 bar strathspey)

1 – 8   1st and 2nd couples dance rights and left while 3rd and 4th do the same.

9 – 16   1st couple followed by 2nd, 3rd and 4th lead down and, passing partners in front, the men dance up on women's side, women on the men's side of the dance (Fig.).

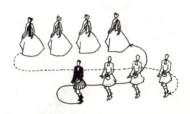

17 – 20 1st and 3rd couples set and cast off one place while 2nd and 4th set and dance up one place.

21 – 24 All set, then 1st and 2nd couples dances 4 hands across half way round, 3rd and 4th do the same.

25 – 28 1st couple giving right hands cross and cast off one place.

29 – 32 Repeat bars 25 – 28 giving left hands.

33 – 36 Repeat bars 25 – 28

37 – 40 Turn partner (giving both hands) one-and-a-half times to own sides at bottom of dance.

Note: dance once only for each couple and only in sets of four.
Source: devised by James Donaldson
Reproduced by kind permission of Kerr's Music Corporation Ltd.

LORD MacLAY'S REEL

Bars   *(40 bar reel)*

1 – 4   1st couple cross over giving right hands and cast down one place (2nd couple moving up) while 4th couple cross over giving right hands and cast up one place (3rd couple moving down).

5 – 8   1st and 4th couples give right hands across to make wheel and dance round for 4 bars finishing in two lines across dance with nearer hands joined, facing top as diagram. (1st couple between 2nd couple and 4th couple between 3rd couple).

1

9 – 16   All pas de basque and coupe step (see p.208) four times.

17 – 24 Reels of Four across dance. Commence by giving right shoulders (Fig. 2). Finish reels by dancing to original places.

2

25 – 32   All join hands in circle, 8 hands round and back.

33 – 36   1st couple cross over giving right hands and cast off one place (2nd couple do not move).

37 – 40   1st couple cross again giving right hands and dance to bottom of set. (2nd, 3rd and 4th couples join hands and move up on last two bars.)

Note:
1. *Before starting reels of four, each couple should note where they are going to finish at sides to be ready for circle.*
2. *In doing reels of four, the two reels should cover each other exactly, i.e. 2 and 3 should cover, and 1 and 4 should cover until each person breaks away to his or her own position at sides.*

Source: dance devised by Miss D. Robertson for the Glasgow Battalion of The Boys Brigade. B.B. Fanfare 1954.

Reproduced by kind permission of Kerr's Music Corporation Ltd.

MRS. MACPHERSON OF INVERAN

(32 bar reel for 3 couples)

1 – 8   *Inveran Reels*

   1 – 4   1st woman dances half a reel of three on the men's side with 2nd and 3rd men, while 1st man dances half a reel of three on the women's side with 2nd and 3rd women.

Bars 1–2

   5 – 8   1st woman dances half a reel of three on her own side with 2nd and 3rd women, while 1st man dances half a reel of three on his own side with 2nd and 3rd men.

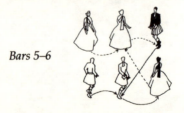

Bars 5–6

2nd and 3rd couples dance normal complete reels of three on the sides (2nd couple dancing out and up, and 3rd couple in and up to start), while 1st couple cross over into the middle of each half-reel.

9 – 12   1st couple turn with the right hand one and a half times, moving down to finish in second place on opposite sides facing out. (2nd couple dance up on bars 9 – 10).

13 – 16   1st couple cast up on opposite sides to above 2nd couple and then, giving left hands, cross over to own sides in second place and stay facing down.

17 – 24   2nd, 1st and 3rd couples dance a grand chain. (2nd couple face across the dance, 1st couple face down and 3rd couple up to start the chain).

25 – 32   Six hands round and back.

Repeat, having passed a couple.

Source: dance devised by John Drewry.

MAIRI'S WEDDING

Bars   (40 bar reel)

1 – 4   1st couple turn with right hand and cast one place on own side (2nd couple move up).

5 – 8   Then turn with left hand to corners.

9 – 12   1st couple dance half reel of four with first corners (the corners changing places).

13 – 16   1st couple dance half reel of four with second corners.

17 – 20   1st couple dance half reel of four with first corners (who are now on other side).

21 – 24   1st couple dance half reel of four with second corners.

25 – 32   Reels of three across, the woman with 2nd couple and the man with 3rd couple.

33 – 40   Six hands round and back.

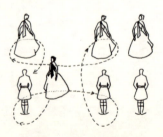

Pattern danced by 1st woman

Pattern danced by 1st man

Note: dancing couple passing left shoulder in centre.
Source: dance devised by James B. Cosh.

J. B. MILNE

1 – 4   1st man and 2nd woman set, approaching, and turn with the right hand back to places.

5 – 8   1st woman and 2nd man do the same.

9 – 12   1st couple set to each other, approaching, and turn with both hands, the man letting go with his left hand first.

13 – 14 1st couple cast off into 2nd place (2nd step up),

15 – 16 And turn, as in Petronella, so that the man is between 3rd couple and woman between 2nd.

17 – 18 1st couple set to each other, while 2nd and 3rd women – and men – change places, giving right hands.

19 – 20 1st couple turn by the right hand three-quarters round to opposite sides, 2nd place, while 2nd and 3rd couples set to partner (Fig. 1).

1

21 – 24 1st couple set to each other and turn three-quarters round by the right hand. Meanwhile 2nd and 3rd couples cross over, giving right hands to partners, then 2nd and 3rd women – and men – set to each other.

25 – 28 1st couple set to each other, facing up and down the dance, and change places, giving right hands, while 2nd and 3rd women – and men – change places, giving right hands, and set to partners.

29 – 30 Continuing, 1st woman casts off, and 1st man casts up, to 2nd place, own sides, while 2nd and 3rd couples cross over, giving right hands to partners (Fig. 2).

2

31 – 32 Taking hands at the sides, all three couples set to partners.

Repeat, having passed a couple.

Source: dance devised by Hugh Foss.
Reproduced by kind permission of Kerr's Music Corporation Ltd.

THE NEW SCOTLAND STRATHSPEY

Bars   *(40 bar strathspey for 4 couples)*

1 – 4   1st and 3rd couples set to partners, and cross over giving right hands, to finish facing down the dance. 2nd and 4th couples face up.

5 – 8   All set to person facing, and turn once, with right hand.

9 – 16   Reels of four at the sides, begin giving right shoulders, finishing in same place (Fig.).

17 –24   Dance eight hands round to left and back.

25 –32   Grand Chain. Begin by men giving right hand to woman on the right.

33 – 34 3rd couple cross back to own side giving right hands, while 1st couple turn once by right hands.

35 – 40 1st couple dance down opposite sides of dance, giving left-right-left hands to 2nd, 3rd and 4th couples (who move up one place) and turn one-and-a-half times by right hand to finish in fourth place.

Repeat until each couple has completed the dance.

Source: devised by Capt. E. G. Elder, Black Watch (RHR).
Reproduced by permission of Scottish National Dance Company, Reading.

THE NEW VIRGINIA REEL

Bars *(A reel for 4 couples in a square set)*

Figure 1

1 – 16 All set to partners and change places with partners giving right hands. Eight hands round and back. All set to partners and change places with partners giving right hands to original positions.

17 – 24 1st and 3rd couples, joining both hands with partners, change places (the men passing back to back), retaining hold of hands, they set using the inside foot first, they slip back to original places with the woman passing back to back and set using the right foot first opening to face in.

25 – 32 2nd and 4th couples repeat bars 17 – 24.

Figure 2

1 – 8 The women dance right hands across once round and then dance round partners by the left back to place.

9 – 16 All set to partners, dance back to back with partners and then set again.

17 – 24 The men dance left hands across once round and then dance round partners by the right back to place.

25 – 32 All repeat bars 9 – 16.

Figure 3

1 – 8 1st man and 3rd woman dance a figure of eight through 2nd couple, and 1st woman and 3rd man dance a figure of eight through 4th couple. Woman dances in front of the man each time, and 2nd and 4th couples stand a little apart.

(see over)

9 – 16   1st and 3rd couples, taking promenade hold with partners, dance half a figure of eight round stationary 4th and 2nd couples. 1st couple begin by passing 4th woman right shoulder. 3rd couple begin by passing 2nd woman right shoulder. 1st and 3rd couples loop round each other in the centre (i.e. men pass each other left shoulders) before dancing out to original places. Couples 4 and 2 stand close to partners.

17 – 24   2nd man and 4th woman dance a figure of eight through 3rd couple, and 2nd woman and 4th man dance similarly through the 1st couple. Woman dances in front of the man each time, and 1st and 3rd couples stand a little apart (Fig.).

25 – 32   2nd and 4th couples, taking promenade hold with partners, dance half a figure of eight round stationary 1st and 3rd couples. 2nd couple begin by passing 1st woman right shoulder. 4th couple begin by passing 3rd woman right shoulder. 2nd and 4th couples loop round each other in the centre (i.e. men pass each other left shoulder). Couples 1 and 3 stand close to partners.

Figure 4
1 – 8   All four women dance rights and lefts within the set, begin-

ning with 1st woman giving right hand to the 2nd woman and 3rd woman giving right hand to the 4th woman.

9 – 16 All four men dance rights and lefts within the set, beginning with 1st man giving right hand to the 4th man and 2nd man giving right hand to the 3rd man.

17 – 32 (As in bars 1 – 16 in Figure 1). All set to partners, change places right hand. Eight hands round and back again. All set to partners, change places right hands to finish in original square set positions.

Note: devised for Eugenia Callander Sharp and the dancers of Alexandria.
Source: dance devised by Anna Holden.

POSTIE'S JIG

Bars   *(32 bar jig for 4 couples)*

1 – 2   1st and 4th couple set.

3 – 4   1st couple cast down and 2nd couple step up, while 4th couple cast up and 3rd couple step down,

5 – 8   1st couple dance half figure of eight round 2nd couple while 4th couple dance half figure of eight round 3rd couple .

9 – 12   1st man and 4th man, 1st woman and 4th woman, with nearer hands joined, cross over, men making arch for women to pass under (Fig. 1). Give 'free' hand to corners and turn, i.e. 1st man to 2nd man and 1st woman to 2nd woman etc. Corners finish to places and 1st couple join nearer hands to face down while 4th couple faces up.

1

13 – 16   Repeat bars 9 – 12 up and down, 4th couple making the arch (Fig. 2 opposite).

17 – 24   Repeat bars 9 – 16.

25 – 28   1st and 4th couples dance half right and lefts.

2

29 – 32 1st and 4th couples turn partners with right hands.

Repeat from new places.

Source: dance devised by Roy Clowes.

THE ROBERTSON RANT

Bars	*(A strathspey danced in square formation)*

1 – 8   Eight hands round and back.

9 – 16   Four women, giving right hands across, wheel half-way round and turn opposite man with left hand, return to places giving right hands across and left to own partners, and turn.

17 – 24   1st and 3rd couples dance figure-of-eight (women begin passing left shoulder).

25 – 32   All set and turn corner partners (Highland setting) (Fig.).

33 – 40   2nd and 4th couples now dance figure-of-eight.

41 – 48   All set to and turn corner partners (Highland setting).

49 – 56   Four women circle to left 4 steps round to face their partner, with whom they set, and turn with both hands (women set with their backs to centre).

57 – 64   Four men circle to right to places, and set and turn their partners (men set with their backs to centre).

65 – 80   Grand chain all round.

Take Allemande formation, turn right and lead off after dancing once round (bars as necessary).

Repeat first tune as required.

Notes:
1. *Bars 9 – 16 are usually danced as a 'double women's chain'*
   In some areas the men start to dance on bar 9 by dancing to partner's place. In other areas the men stand for two bars and then continue to dance.
2. *Bars 17 – 24: the 'figure of eight' is a reel of four.*
   In some areas the men begin by setting on bars 17 – 18, in others they stand still.
3. *Bars 25 – 28: the 'Highland setting' is Highland Schottische (see p. 45). It is customary to turn corner partners twice with both hands on bars 29 – 32.*
4. *Bars 49 – 52: it is customary for women to pull right shoulders back in the middle of the set at the end of the circle to finish facing partners.*
5. *Bars 65 – 80. The grand chain is normally danced in eight bars (one step to each hand) and then, taking allemande hold with partners, all dance round the set once anticlockwise and, at the end, the men bring their partners round into the middle of the set and retain hold of partners with the right hand for the final bow and curtsy.*

Source: dance devised in 1949 by Mrs Douglas Winchester (Maidie Logie Robertson).

THE ROTHESAY RANT

Bars   *(A jig for 4 couples in a square set)*

1 – 4   Giving right hand to partner, change places with two skip change of step. Retain hold and give left hand to the next person so that all are joined in a circle, women facing in, men facing out, set right and left (Fig.).

5 – 8   Dropping right hands, change places with person on left hand to join in circle again, men facing in and women facing out. Set right and left, women turning by the right to face the centre on bar 8 and forming square set.

9 – 12   1st couple with 3rd couple, half ladies' chain.

13 – 16   1st couple with 3rd couple, half rights and lefts.

17 – 24   Similarly, 2nd and 4th couples dance half ladies' chain, followed by half rights and lefts.

25 – 32   Eight hands round and back again.

Repeat from new position.

Note: half ladies' chain is started each time from the sides of the set, as in bar 9. Each couple has progressed one place clockwise at the end of every 32 bars
Source: dance devised by Anna Holden.
Reproduced by kind permission of the Birmingham Branch, RSCDS.

THE SAINT JOHN RIVER

Bars   *(32 bar strathspey for 4 couples)*

1 – 8   1st woman casts off one place, crosses and casts behind 3rd man, crosses and casts behind 4th woman and crosses to finish below 4th man on opposite side of the dance; 1st man follows his partner to finish below 4th woman on opposite side of the dance.

9 – 16   1st couple, with nearer hands joined, dances up under the arch formed by 4th couple, turns one and a half times with two hands, then dances up under the arch formed by 2nd couple, finishing in 1st place on own side of the dance, 4th couple holds the arch on bars 9 – 10 only and 2nd couple makes the arch on bars 15 – 16.

17 – 24   1st couple leads down the middle and up, followed by 2nd, 3rd and 4th couples; 2nd couple dances up for two bars, leads down for two bars, up for two bars and dances down to place for two bars; 3rd couple dances up for three bars, leads down for one bar, up for one bar and dances down to place for three bars; 4th couple dances up for four bars to meet at the top of the set but does not join hands, then casts out and dances down to place for four bars.

25 – 28   All four couples dance back-to-back (Fig.).

(see over)

29 – 32   1st couple wends its way down own side of the dance, changing place with 2nd couple with right hands. 3rd couple with left hands and 4th couple with right hands to finish in fourth place, 1st man and 4th woman making polite turns.

Repeat with new couple.

Note: 'The Saint John River' won first place in a contest to select a Scottish country dance to commemorate Canada's Centennial in 1967. Organised by the Deep River Branch of The Royal Scottish Country Dance Society, this group published the twenty-one dances submitted in Scottish Country Dances – A Centennial Collection. *Unfortunately this publication is now out of print. Music for the dance was recorded in 1970, helping to make 'The Saint John River' popular with Scottish country dancers around the world.*

Source: dance devised by Pru Edwards, 1966.

SETON'S CEILIDH BAND

Bars   *(64 bar jig for 4 couples)*

1 – 8 1st couple cross over giving right hands, cast off behind 2nd couple (who move up on bars 3 – 4), dance in front of 3rd couple (who move up on bars 5 – 6) and behind 4th couple (who move up on bars 7 – 8) to finish in fourth place on opposite sides.

9 – 16 1st woman dances a reel of three with 3rd and 4th men while 1st man dances a reel of three with 3rd and 4th women. 1st couple dance up *between* 4th couple to begin the reels (Fig. 1.).

1

17 – 24 1st couple repeat bars 1 – 8 dancing up the set to original places.

25 – 32 1st woman dances a reel of three with 2nd and 3rd women while 1st man dances a reel of three with 2nd and 3rd men. 1st couple dance down *between* 2nd couple to begin the reels.

33 – 36 1st couple cross over giving right hands and cast off one place to finish between first corners – right hands joined with partner and left hands joined with corners. 2nd couple move up on bars 35 - 36.

(see over)

37 – 38   All balance in line (Fig. 2).

39 – 40   1st couple turn with right hands to finish between 2nd corners.

41 – 42   All balance in line.

43 – 44   1st couple dance down behind 3rd couple on opposite sides

(Fig. 3).

45 – 48   1st couple lead up to the top and cross over to finish on own sideline facing down. 2nd couple move down on bars 47 – 48 and face up.

49 – 50   1st and 2nd women change places giving right hands while 1st and 2nd men do the same.

51 – 52   2nd and 1st couples cross over giving left hand to partner.

53 – 56   1st couple repeat bars 49 – 52 with 3rd couple – 1st woman changing places with 3rd man and 1st man with 3rd woman.

57 – 60   1st couple repeat bars 49 – 52 with 4th couple.

61 – 64   All four couples turn partner with right hand one and a half times to own sides.

Repeat with a new top couple.

Source: dance devised by Bruce Fordyce.

SHIFTIN' BOBBINS

Bars   *(32 bar reel)*

1 – 2   1st couple cross giving right hands moving down the set to
finish back to back facing 2nd couple on the opposite sides.
2nd couple step up (Fig. 1).

1

3 – 4   Giving hands as in double triangles, 1st, 2nd and 3rd
couples set.

5 – 8   1st couple dance out on opposite side and cast up, meet,
give nearer hands and dance down to places (Fig. 2).

2

9 – 12   1st woman with 2nd and 3rd men dances right hands across
while 1st man with 2nd and 3rd women dances left hands
across once round.

13 – 16   1st couple meet, and giving inside hands, lead down centre
followed by 2nd and 3rd couples.

17 – 24 All turn about and 3rd couple lead back, casting off so all dance hands across with opposite hand. Now back at Fig. 2, with first couple facing up.

25 – 28 1st couple, giving inside hands, lead up and cast off to second place on the opposite sides.

29 – 32 1st couple dance half a figure of eight round 2nd couple to finish in second place.

Repeat from second place.

Source: dance devised by Roy Clowes.

THE THIRTYTWOSOME REEL

Dancers take up positions as in Fig. 1.

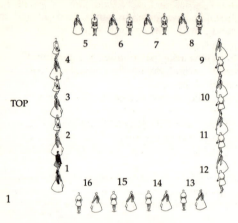

1 – 8	Thirtytwo hands round and back. Finish ready for
9 – 12	Double right hands across (women in the middle) (Fig. 2).

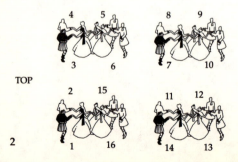

244

13 – 16   Double left hands across (men in the middle)
Finish ready for

17 – 24   All set to partners twice; and turn once with both hands joined (eight pas de basques)

25 – 40   Grand Chain.
Finish in starting positions, as Fig. 1.
Bars 9 – 40 are virtually four eightsome reels, danced in the corners of the square.
Note: in the last two or three bars of the grand chain 6th man and 3rd woman require to speed up (similarly 2nd, 10th and 14th men, and 7th, 11th and 15th women). At the same time, 3rd man and 6th woman require to slow down (similarly 7th, 11th and 15th men and 6th, 10th and 14th women).

1 – 8   Twentyeight hands round and back, while 1st, 2nd, 3rd and 4th women dance into the middle using a suitable setting step*, and finish facing partners (Fig. 3)

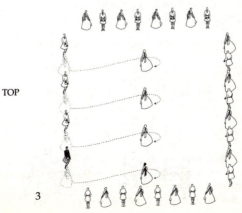

TOP

3

(see over)

(* e.g. four pas de basques moving forward, two pas de basques turning right about, and four spring points).

9 – 12 1st, 2nd, 3rd and 4th women set to partners (who also set), and turn with two hands, finishing facing 12th, 11th, 10th and 9th men. (During bars 11 and 12 these men step forward right, left, right, left.)

13 – 16 1st, 2nd, 3rd and 4th women set to these men (who also set) and turn with two hands. Women finish facing partners.

17 – 24 1st, 2nd, 3rd and 4th women dance a reel of three with their partners and opposite men. The men finish back in place. The women finish in the middle of the set facing partners, (Fig. 4).

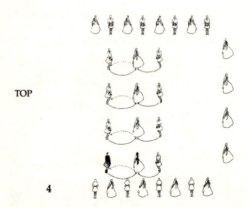

TOP

4

25 – 32 Twenty-eight hands round and back, while 1st, 2nd, 3rd and 4th women using a suitable setting step and keeping in line, move 90° in a clockwise direction to finish facing 5th, 6th, 7th and 8th men. Using this manoeuvre 3rd and 4th women move backward, while 2nd and 1st women move forward (Fig. 5).

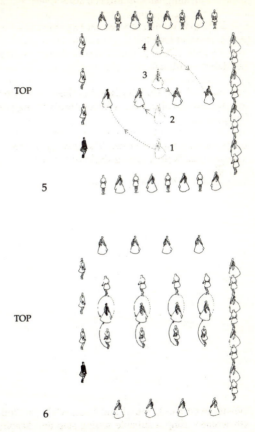

33 – 40 1st, 2nd, 3rd and 4th women set to, and turn 5th, 6th, 7th and 8th men and 16th, 15th, 14th and 13th, as in bars 13 – 16.

41 – 48   1st, 2nd, 3rd and 4th women dance reels of three with these men, all finishing back in place. This is easily accomplished if 4th woman leaves the reel of three on bar 45, 3rd woman on bar 46, 2nd woman on bar 47, and 1st woman on bar 48 (Fig. 6 on previous page).

49 – 384   The dance continues with the figures being danced in turn by 5th, 6th, 7th and 8th woman = 9th, 10th 11th and 12th and 13th, 14th, 15th and 16th; then 1st, 2nd, 3rd and 4th men = 5th, 6th, 7th and 8th = 9th, 10th 11th and 12th and 13th, 14th, 15th and 16th.

1 – 40   As for the first 40 bars of the dance.
Finish in the original square set.

Source: unknown. Collected by W. J. Ireland.

A TRIP TO BAVARIA

Bars   *(32 bar reel for 4 couples)*

1 – 2   Couples in 1st and 4th positions cross right hand, while those in 2nd and 3rd positions dance 4 hands across, half way right hand (Fig. 1).

1

TOP

3 – 4   All dance up or down the sides of the dance, changing places left hand (1st and 2nd position and 3rd and 4th position).

5 – 6   As bars 1 and 2.

7 – 8   As bars 3 and 4.

9 – 16 As bars 1 to 8 inclusive.

17 – 18 1st couple facing down, 2nd facing up, set. (i.e. man to man, woman to woman).

19 – 20 1st cross down to 2nd place, while 2nd couple dance up to 1st place.

21 – 22 1st couple facing down, 3rd facing up, set. (man to woman, woman to man).

23 – 24   1st couple cross down to 3rd place, while 3rd couple dance up to 2nd place

25 – 26   1st couple facing down, 4th couple facing up, set. (man to man , woman to woman)

27 – 28   1st couple cross down to 4th place opposite sides, while 4th couple dance up to 3rd place.

All are now on the opposite side of the dance as shown in Fig. 2:

2

29 – 30   Joining hands, all advance (2 skip steps). Here, 1st couple deftly: drop hands, and with the right hand (which the woman already has 'free') turn to join hands again with the others, and

31 – 32   All retire (2 skip steps).

Source: dance devised by James MacGregor-Brown c. 1960.

THE WHITE HEATHER JIG

Bars   *(40 bar jig)*

1 – 4   1st couple turn with right hand and cast off to second place. (2nd couple step up).

5 – 8   1st couple turn with left hand one and a half times and finish back to back between 2nd couple, 1st woman facing 2nd man and 1st man facing 2nd woman.

9 – 16   1st and 2nd couples a reel of four across (1st couple pass right shoulder to finish facing first corner) (Fig.).

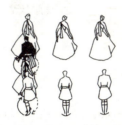

17 – 24   Turn corner with right hand, partner with left hand, second corner with right hand and turn partner with left hand to finish back to back between 3rd couple (1st woman facing 3rd man and 1st man the 3rd woman).

25 – 32   1st and 3rd couples a reel of four across, 1st man particularly a full reel of four. 3rd couple finish in 2nd place. (1st couple meet in centre between 3rd and 4th couples).

33 – 36   1st couple turn with left hand and cast down on own side. (4th couple step up).

37 – 40   1st couple turn with right hand.

Source: dance devised by James B. Cosh.

Ceilidh & Party Dances

Ceilidh is the Gaelic word for a gathering at which spontaneous singing, verse, dancing and music takes place, usually in a person's house. However, there is very little connection between today's 'ceilidh' dancing and that described by the original use of the word.

Ceilidh dancing today usually refers to couple dancing or old-time dancing as opposed to country dancing in sets of couples. Many of the dances are traditional (devised in the last century or earlier) while others, such as the 'Lambeth Walk' or the 'Palais Glide', are more modern. Many of the more recent dances were originally devised as competition sequence dances, with instructions which had very precise foot positions similar to Highland dances. Some of theses dances proved to be so popular that they found their way in the ballroom with greatly simplified instructions; this is one of the reasons why there are so many variations of these dances recorded. It must be emphasised that the instructions on the following pages are those collected by various teachers and so there are bound to be regional variations.

Explanations of the terminology used in these instruction are as follows:

Line of dance: an anti-clockwise direction round the room

Against the line of dance: a clockwise direction round the room

Ballroom hold: couple face each other, close together; the man places his right hand around partner's waist while she places her left hand on his right shoulder. They join their other hands at shoulder height almost at arm's length (see Fig.).

Two videos, *Step We Ceilidh*, *Step We Ceilidh 2* which show many of the ceilidh/party dances) are available from Independent Video Productions, Devon Bank House, Fishcross, Alloa FK10 3JE. (tel. 01259-724169).

The following dances are recorded on one CD: *'Music for the Collins Pocket Reference Scottish Country Dancing (Vol. One)'* [RSCDS - CD8].

BLUEBELL POLKA

In couples facing line of dance, man's right arm round
woman's waist, woman's left hand on man's shoulder.

Bars

1 – 2   Starting with outside foot, (with hops) point side, point in,
point in front, point in.

3 – 4   Woman crosses to the other side of the man with a run, run
run hop.

5 – 8   Repeat from opposite side, finishing woman in front of man.
Man facing line of dance.

9 – 12   Now in ballroom hold both run run run hop, twice.

13 – 16   Turn with four step hops along the line of dance to finish
opening out. Ready to start again.

Music: own tune
Source: dance originally devised by Johnny Coombs. Collected by Johan
Maclean.

BOSTON TWO STEP

In couples facing line of dance, nearer hands joined.
Men on inside, start with outside foot.

Bars

1 – 2   Pas de basque away from each other then towards each other.

3 – 4   3 walking steps forward (start with outside foot), turning inwards on the 4th step.

5 – 8   Repeat back to place: pas de basque, 'walk, walk, walk and turn'.

9 – 10 Facing each other, man back to the centre, both hands joined pas de basque (man starts with left foot, woman right foot).

11 – 12 Chasse to man's left, finish in ballroom hold (step close, step close).

13 – 16 Ballroom hold, waltz round opening out to start again.

Music: 6/8 time
Source: dance originally devised by Tom Walton. Collected by Barbara Gibbons

BRITANNIA TWO STEP

In lines facing the line of dance. Man between two
women, or woman between two men.

Bars   *(Dance for 3 people)*

1 – 2   Starting with left foot all place left heel forward, toe to
           instep of right foot, and skip change of step to the left.

3 – 4   Place right heel forward, toe to instep of left foot, and skip
           change of step to the right.

5 – 8   Walk forward left, right, left, swing right, walk backward
           right, left, right swing left.

9 – 12   Two pas de basque steps on the spot and two pas de basque
           steps to turn outside under centre person's arms.

13 – 16   Walk forward, left, right, left, swing right, walk backward,
           right, left, right, swing left.

           This may be danced progressively, i.e. on the last 3 steps, the
           centre person dances forward to join the next line.

Music: any 6/8 tune
Source: collected by Johan Maclean.

CANADIAN BARN DANCE

In couples facing line of dance, nearer hands joined.
Start with outside foot.

Bars

1 – 4   Move forward with 3 runs and a hop. Repeat moving backwards.

5 – 8   Move to side away from partner with same step and clap on the hop. Move back to partner and join up with ballroom hold.

9 – 12   3 runs and a hop in line of dance. 3 runs and a hop against line of dance. (Side together side hop.)

13 – 16   Turning and progressing round the room with step hop open out ready to begin again.

This may be danced progressively, i.e. after moving away from partner and clapping, instead of moving back to partner, the man moves diagonally forward and at the same time the woman moves diagonally back to meet a new partner with ballroom hold and continue.

Music: 2/4 pipe march
Source: dance originally devised by B. Durrands. Collected by Mary Stoker.

CIRCLE WALTZ

One big circle facing the middle, men having their partners on their right, all joining hands and beginning with the right foot.

Bars

1 – 2   Balance forward and back.

3 – 4   Men, releasing their partner's hand, with both hands swing the woman on their left in front of them to finish on their right.

5 – 16   Repeat this *three* more times and hold onto the woman facing her and taking ballroom hold, stand side towards centre of room.

17 – 20 Men begin left foot, partner right foot, and moving towards the centre, step close, step close, then – step close step.

21 – 24 Repeat but moving towards the wall.

25 – 32 Waltz round the room, reforming the circle to begin again.

Note: as a variation for bars 17 – 24, take 2 steps to the centre, dropping hands, turn away from partner right round and meet again; then repeat towards the wall.
Music: medley of waltzes
Source: dance originally devised by Alex Moore. Collected by Mary Stoker

ELEPHANT WALK

**In couples facing round room, facing each other, man
with back to centre.**

Bars

1   All begin right foot. Point right foot to side , no weight, tap
     beside left foot, no weight, repeat point to side then close to
     left foot.

2   Repeat above with left foot.

3   Point right foot diagonally back, no weight, tap beside left
     foot, no weight, repeat point diagonally back and then close
     to left foot.

4   Repeat with left foot.

5   Lift right knee and touch with left elbow, point right foot to
     side, no weight. Lift right knee and touch with left elbow,
     close right foot beside left foot.

6   Lift left knee and touch with right elbow, point left foot to
     side, no weight. Lift left knee and touch with right elbow,
     close left foot beside right foot.

7   Kick right leg across left leg, close right foot to left foot. Kick
     left leg across right leg, close left foot to right foot.

8   With feet together, jump sideways to the left to face new
     partner; nod to new partner and clap own hands.

Music: Laughing Samba
Source: collected by Mary Stoker.

EVA THREE STEP

In couples facing line of dance. Nearer hands joined.
Start with outside foot.

Bars

1 – 2   Walk forward three steps and point toe to floor.

3 – 4   Woman crosses in front of partner three steps – left, right
left and point right as man crosses behind her for three steps
right, left, right and point left and rejoin hands.

5 – 6   Man crosses in front of partner three steps – left, right, left
and point right as woman crosses behind him for three
steps – right, left, right and point left and rejoin hands (no
turns on crossings).

7 – 8   Walk back three steps – right, left, right and point, man left,
lady right to finish taking ballroom hold.

9 – 10   Two side steps along line of dance.

11 – 12   Two side steps against line of dance.

13 – 16   Two complete waltz turns along the line of dance to finish
opening out with near hands joined.

Music: any 6/8 tune
Source: dance originally devised by Sydney W. Painter for his daughter,
Eva. Collected by Johan Maclean.

FRIENDLY WALTZ

In couples facing line of dance, nearer hands joined.
Start with outside foot.

Bars

1   Balance forward (men step left close right).

2   Balance back (men step right close left).

3 – 4   2 waltz steps turning away from partner.

5 – 6   Repeat balance forward and back.

7 – 8   Waltz, turning slightly away from partner then towards, joining both hands with partner.

9   Balance sideways along line of dance. (Step close).

10   Balance sideways against line of dance. (Step close).

11 – 12 Woman progresses to man to her left by turning under her partner's left arm with 2 waltz steps, finishing in ballroom hold while man balances along line of dance and hesitates.

13 – 16 In ballroom hold waltz round with new partner. Opening out to start again.

Music: any waltz
Source: dance originally devised by B.M. and T. Edney. Collected by Alastair Aitkenhead.

GAY GORDONS

In couples facing line of dance. Allemande hold, i.e. men holds partner's right hand with his right hand behind her right shoulder and holds her left hand in his left hand about waist level. Begin with outside foot.

Bars

1 – 4   Walk forward 4 steps, turning on the fourth. Keeping hand in allemande position (but now left arm is high and right arm is low), walk backwards for 4 steps in line of dance.

5 – 8   4 steps forward against line of dance, turning on 4, and 4 steps backwards.

9 – 12   Face partner taking right hand, men walk forward in line of dance turning partner under right arm.

13 – 16   Ballroom hold, polka round and open out ready to begin again.

Music: any march
Source: collected by Mary Stoker.

HESITATION WALTZ

In couples facing line of dance starting on outside foot, nearer hands joined.

Bars

1 – 2   Step swing forward, and step back on inside foot (touch floor with outside foot).

3 – 4   Repeat bars 1 – 2.

5 – 8   Starting again with outside foot walk forward in the rhythm 1-2-3 and -4.

9 – 12   Repeat 5 – 8 in a backward direction starting on inside foot, finishing facing partner in ballroom hold.

13 – 16   Waltz for four steps turning along the line of dance opening out with nearer hands joined.

Music: any waltz
Source: dance originally devised by John Evans. Collected by Johan Maclean.

HIGHLAND SCHOTTISCHE

In couples round room. Ballroom hold. Men with back to centre of room. Man begins left foot, woman right foot.

Bars

1 – 4   Highland Schottische setting steps in line of dance then against line of dance (see p. 45 for this step).

5 – 6   Common Schottische setting steps with half a turn on the hop at the end of each setting (see p. 44 for this step).

7 – 8   Step hop placing the free foot on the hopping leg and turning as you dance. Man may have hands on partner's waist and she has hands on partner's shoulders.

Music: Orange and Blue
Source: collected by Mary Stoker.

KELVINGROVE TWO STEP

Couples round the room, facing partner. Men with back to centre.

Bars

1 –2 Men start left foot. All retire 4 steps, clap on the last step.

3 –4 All advance 4 steps.

5 –8 Taking both hands, step to side along line of dance. Men left foot; cross right foot over; step left; and point right in the air. Women right foot, cross left foot over; step right and point left in the air. 'Step cross step lift'. Repeat other foot against line of dance

9 – 10 With pas de basque, turn away from partner right round.

11 – 12 Meet partner, taking both hands set on the spot.

13 – 16 Taking ballroom hold, polka round, ready to start again.

Music: own tune
Source: collected by Nan Lawson.

LAMBETH WALK

In couples facing line of dance both arms are raised, elbows bent, hands towards chest, thumbs up. Man begins left foot, partner right foot.

Bars

1 – 4   Walk forward for 8 steps; swing left shoulder forward with left foot and similarly right shoulder with right foot.

5 – 8   Each linking left arm with partner walk round with 8 steps keeping right arm in thumbs up position. Turn to face line of dance on last 2 steps; lady walks for 6 steps and marks time facing line of dance on 7 and 8.

9 –10   Man links nearer arm with partner and begins left foot, (partner right foot). Step left foot, step right foot, step left foot, then weight back onto right foot and forward onto left foot.

11 – 12   Step right foot, step left foot, step right foot then weight back onto left foot and forward onto right foot. This is really a rocking movement.

13   Partners move away from each other, man towards the centre, lady towards outside of circle. Step to side with left foot cross right foot over left foot.

14   Step to side with left foot turning to face partner, bend and slap both knees.

15 – 16   Walk towards partner closing right foot to left foot, on 4 swing right arm over shoulder pointing back with thumb and shouting 'oi!'. Face forward to begin again.

Music: own tune
Source: collected by Mary Stoker

LOMOND WALTZ

In couples round the room, in ballroom hold. Man with back to the centre.

Bars

1 – 2   Step left close right to third position, i.e. right instep touching left heel, and step left again.

3 – 4   2 gliding steps back, right foot then left foot.

5 – 6   Step close step beginning right foot.

7 – 8   2 gliding steps forward, left foot then right foot. Dancers have now moved in a square formation and are back to the starting position.

9 – 12   Release partner, keeping own hands at shoulder height, walk in a circle on own; man by the left, partner by the right (4 walking steps).

13 – 20   Face partner taking hands; balance forward and back and change side turning woman under man's left hand and face each other repeat back to place, finish with both hands joined.

21 – 24   Man steps left foot along line of dance, crosses right foot over and points left foot diagonally forward; he then brings it into the instep of the right foot and pivots a quarter turn to the right. (Partner steps right foot, cross left foot point right foot and pivot to left.)

25 – 28   Repeat the step against the line of dance.

29 – 32   Ballroom hold, waltz round to open out ready to begin again.

Music: Loch Lomond
Source: dance originally devised by Botham. Collected by Mary Stoker.

MILITARY TWO STEP

In couples facing line of dance, nearer hands joined. Start with outside foot.

Bars

1 – 4   Place foot forward on heel then reach back and place same foot on toe, 4 walks forward changing hands and turning to face opposite direction on 4.

5 – 8   Repeat in opposite direction, i.e. against line of dance.

9 – 10   Face partner with both hands joined, set with 2 pas de basque (man starts with left foot).

11 – 12   Man turns partner under right arm.

13 – 16   Ballroom hold, quick waltz or two step turning round and progressing round room, open out ready to begin again.

Music: any 6/8 tune
Source: dance originally devised by James Finnigan. Collected by Mary Stoker.

MISSISSIPPI DIP

Couples in ballroom hold, man with back to centre of room. Man starts with left foot, partner right foot. Steps are given for the man, partner on opposite foot.

Bars

1   3 steps back towards centre. Left, right, left, point right foot back. (4 quick steps).

2   Sway left along line of dance, sway right against line of dance. (2 slow steps).

3   4 steps towards wall. Left, right, left, right. (4 quick steps).

4   Sway left along line of dance, sway right against line of dance. (2 slow steps).

5   Chasse to left along line of dance. Left, right, left, with sway to left. (Quick, quick, slow).

6   Chasse to right against line of dance. Right, left, right with sway to right. (Quick, quick, slow).

7 – 8   Rotary waltz finish in promenade hold and facing line of dance. (Quick + quick, quick + quick, quick + quick, quick + quick).

9   Left foot along line of dance, forward right foot with plie or dip and point. (Slow slow).

10   Left foot forward (short step) swivel on balls of feet, half turn to right, swivel half turn to left. (Slow. Quick quick).

11   Left foot along line of dance, forward right foot with plie or dip and point. (Slow, slow).

(see over)

12   Left foot forward (short step) swivel on balls of feet half turn to right, swivel half turn to left. (Slow, quick, quick).

13   Chasse to left along line of dance. Left, right. left, with sway to left. (Quick quick slow).

14   Chasse to right against line of dance. Right, left, right with sway to right. (Quick, quick. Slow).

15 – 16   Rotary waltz, finish ballroom hold, ready to start again. (quick + quick, quick + quick, quick + quick, quick + quick).

Music: own tune or any hoe down
Source: dance originally devised by Charles Wood. Collected by Nan Lawson.

PALAIS GLIDE

Lines of 4 or more facing round the room with hands joined behind the back.

1st phrase
Left foot forward to tap heel on floor (no weight on it).
Step back on left foot.
Step to side with right foot.
Step in front with left foot.
Right foot forward to tap heel on floor (no weight on it).

2nd phrase
Step back on right foot.
Step to side with left foot.
Step in front with right foot.
Left foot forward to tap heel on floor (no weight on it).

3rd phrase
Step back on left foot.
Step to side with right foot.

4th phrase
Step forward on left foot and hop swinging right leg forward.
Cross right leg over left leg hopping and swinging left leg forward.
Cross left leg over right leg hopping and swinging right leg forward.
Cross right leg over left leg hopping and swinging left leg forward.
Step on left foot and swing right leg back bending forward at the same time.
Swing right leg forward straightening up, 3 runs forward finishing on right leg ready to begin again with heel tapping with left foot.

Music: Poor Little Angeline or similar
Source: dance originally devised by Charles J. Daniels. Collected by Mary Stoker.

PRIDE OF ERIN WALTZ

In couples facing line of dance, nearer hands joined.

Bars

1 – 4   Point or swing outside leg forward/back, step, close, step and turn to face opposite direction.

5 – 8   Repeat to original positions.

9 – 12   Face each other, both hands joined men back to the centre. Then men step left foot over right foot and point right foot against line of dance. Step right foot over left foot and point left foot along line of dance. (Women use opposite foot).

13 – 16   Solo turn away from each other, then *either* solo turn back *or* continue solo turn away a second time.

17 – 20   Balance (both hands joined) towards and away from partner, and turn partner under her right arm (man's left), to change sides.

21 – 24   Repeat to place.

25 – 28   2 side steps along line of dance. 2 side steps against line of dance.

29 – 32   Ballroom hold, waltz round, opening out to start again.

Music: any good Irish waltz tunes of 32 bars
Source: dance originally devised by Charles Wood. Collected by Barbara Gibbons.

St. Bernard's Waltz

Couples in ballroom hold, men back to the centre.
Men start with the left foot, women with right foot.

Bars

1 – 4   Step left foot close right foot, step left foot close right foot, step left foot close right foot with a light stamp, and lightly stamp left foot. (Side, side, side, stamp, stamp.)

5 – 8   Step right foot close left foot, step right foot close left foot, without weight, step back left foot, step back right foot. (towards centre).

9 – 12   Step forward left foot, step forward right foot, (towards wall) lady turns under the man's left hand.

13 – 16   Waltz round, ready to begin again.

Music: old-time waltz
Source: collected by Barbara Gibbons.

SHEENA'S SAUNTER

One large circle, facing in, men have their partners on their right, hands joined.

Bars

1 – 4   All walk towards centre, 4 steps. All retire to place, 4 steps.

5 – 8   Repeat.

9 – 12   Men only with 4 walking steps advance towards centre and retire to place.

13 – 16   Women repeat, finish facing partners.

17 – 24   Grand chain: give right hand to the person you are facing to change places, left to the next and so on for 7 steps (men dance round anti-clockwise and women clockwise): on the last right hand, men take their new partner into promenade hold (hands crossed in front), all facing line of dance.

25 – 32   All dance round the room opening out to start again.

Music: any march
Source: collected by Peter Knight.

THE SOCIAL SWING

Nearer hands joined in lines of any chosen number (e.g. 6, 8, 10, or 12) across the floor all facing the same direction.

Bars

1 – 4   Starting with right foot walk forward 1, 2, 3 and turn, walk backwards (in same direction 1, 2, 3, 4).

5 – 8   Repeat bars 1 – 4.

9 – 10   Cross right step left cross and hop on right (moving to the left).

11 – 12   Repeat moving to right.

13 – 14   Set once (pas de basque) right and left.

15 – 16   Step forward right and hop. Step forward left and hop.

Music: as 'Gay Gordons'
Source: dance originally devised by Ken Fuller. Collected by Johan Maclean.

STERN POLKA

Couples round the room. Ballroom hold, men with back to centre.

Bars

A –
16 bars
Polka round the room, opening out to face the line of dance.

B –
16 bars
Man takes partner round the waist, his right hand in her right hand, resting on her right hip, woman's left hand on man's right shoulder; he places his left hand on left shoulder of man in front: march round circle.

C –
16 bars
Let go of partner. Man faces inwards. Man stands and claps using *both* hands in rhythm as in note below: own thighs once, own hands twice, then hand of both neighbours at head-height (own right to right hand neighbour's left, left to left hand neighbour's right), then own hands above own head once. Repeat to end of C music.

Meanwhile, women dance round outside of circle.

When A music begins again, men turn to face out ready to polka with a new partner.

At the end of the last time through, bands usually play 16 bars of A music so as to finish with a polka.

Note: clapping rhythm goes: (still in 2/4 rhythm) 1 – 2 -and 1 – 2, 1 – 2 – and 1 – 2, etc.

Music: original tune (essential), 2/4 time in 3 sections
Source: dance originally devised by B.M. and T. Edney. Collected by Barbara Gibbons.

THE SUZUKI CIRCLE

One circle round the room, men have their partner on their right.

Bars

1 – 8   All advance with 4 skip change of step and retire back to place.

9 – 12   Women advance for 2 skip change and retire to place.

13 – 16   Men dance in for 2 steps, turn and dance back to face their partners.

17 – 20   All set twice (pas de basque)

21 – 24   All turn partners with right hand and finish in promenade hold (hands crossed in front) facing line of dance.

25 – 32   All promenade with skip change of step and finish with partner on right.

33 – 40   All taking hands, dance 'hands round' to the left in a circle for 16 steps.

Note: this dance may become progressive by the man dancing to the woman behind his partner on bars 15 – 16. This is an adaptation of the original English 'Circassian Circle'. It was introduced by staff at the St. Andrews Summer School of The Royal Scottish Country Dance Society to a group of over 200 young musicians attending the annual Suzuki conference who wished to have an insight into Scottish Country dancing. This dance is a simple 40-bar arrangement using some basic steps and formations of Scottish country dancing.

Music: any suitable reel
Source: collected initially by Alastair Aitkenhead in Sweden in 1949.

SWEDISH MASQUERADE

In couples facing line of dance, nearer hands joined and start with outside foot. Danced in 3 parts. Slow march, waltz and polka, 16 bars each.

Bars

**Slow
March**

1 – 8   8 walking steps forward along line of dance closing on 8th step to change direction.

9 – 16   8 walking steps against line of dance to starting position, turning on 8th step to face line of dance.

Waltz

1 – 4   Nearer hands joined. Balance away from partner then towards partner. Repeat; away, towards.

5 – 8   Ballroom hold, waltz round twice

9 – 12   Repeat 1 – 4, balance away, towards, away, towards.

13 – 16   Repeat 5 – 8, ballroom hold, waltz round twice.

Polka   As for waltz, but polka step for turning instead of waltz step.

Repeat from slow march all the way through.

Music: own music
Source: collected by Nan Lawson.

La Va

In couples round the room. Ballroom hold. Men with back to the centre of the room.

Man hops on right foot, steps forward on left foot crossing in front of partner, closes right foot to left foot, steps onto left foot as he completes half turn to be on opposite side of partner and points right foot in line of dance: then hops on left foot, steps forward on right foot and closes left foot to right foot, steps onto right foot and points left foot forward in line of dance. He repeats these 2 steps another 3 times, (4 complete turns).

The lady meanwhile hops on left foot, steps forward on right foot, closes left foot to right foot, steps onto right foot and points left foot forward in line of dance: Then hops on right foot, crossing in front of partner, closes right foot to left foot, steps onto right foot as she completes half turn to be back on original side and points right foot forward in line of dance. Repeat these 2 steps another 3 times, (4 complete turns).

(Dancer on inside moves over in front of partner dancing half turn, then dances next step straight.)

Man hopping on right foot, and lady on left foot, dance 'hop, step and close', hop, step and close (these 2 steps in line of dance). Hop step and close step point (this step with a half turn). Repeat this sequence (4 steps) another 3 times.

Repeat all the way through from the beginning.

Music: La Varsovienne
Source: collected by Nan Lawson

VELETA

In couples round the room, facing each other. Both hands joined. Man with back to centre. Man starts with left foot and woman with right foot.

Bars

1 – 4   Step sideways in line of dance and swing other leg across. Step against line of dance and swing other leg across; then moving in line of dance 'step close step'.

5 – 8   Repeat, beginning against line of dance.

9 – 12   Step close step in line of dance, then against line of dance.

13 – 16   Ballroom hold, then waltz round.

Music: waltz time, own tune
Source: collected by Mary Stoker.

VIRGINIA REEL

Longwise set with 4 or more couples facing each other,
men with left side towards top of room.

Bars

1 – 8   Hold hands in line, all begin left foot. Advance and retire;
i.e. 4 walks forward, 4 walks back. Repeat.

9 – 16   All turn partner right hand, back to place, (8 walking steps)
all turn partner left hand, back to place, (8 walking steps).

17 – 20 All turn partner both hands, back to place (8 walking steps).

21 – 24 All dance back to back, passing partner right shoulder and
left shoulder (8 walking steps).

25 – 32 Top couple joining both hands chasse or slip step down the
middle for 8 counts while side couples clap in rhythm, then
top couple chasse or slip step up the middle for 8 counts
while side couples clap in rhythm.

33 – 36 Top couple separate, turn outwards, and travel to the
bottom of the set, their own sides following (8 walking
steps).

37 – 40 Top couple join hands to form an arch, the other dancers
pass under the arch and back to place; 2nd couple now
become top couple.

Repeat until all the couples in the set have become top
couple.

Music: any good hoe down
Source: collected by Mary Stoker.

Appendix: Hints on Reeling

There are a number of important differences between the dance techniques explained in this book, which would be encountered at RSCDS functions, and what you would expect to find at a 'reeling' party or Highland ball. Variations in general technique and for specific dances are outlined below.

Formations

It is important to realise that dances are made up of different formations (usually of eight bars) or of half formations (four bars) and that a dance is usually four formations, or combination of half formations, to make a total of 32 bars of music. So, by learning a few basic formations, it is possible to dance many dances, simply by combining formations in a different sequence.

Note that in a figure-of-eight formation, two people stand while one person moves; if all three move it is a reel of three. Also, the hands across formation is sometimes referred to by reelers as 'teapots'.

Sets

Sets are usually counted in five or six couples. However, if there are more dancers than this taking part in any particular dance, especially going all the way down the line, the bottom couples will not get a turn at the top.

Steps

Remember that both pas de basque and skip change of step take one bar of music whereas there are two walking steps to one bar of music. To dance pas de basque and skip change of step all night is very tiring, so lilting in time to the music is the usual way to preserve stamina; continue to count the bars when setting ('1-2-3 and…'), but the feet should hardly leave the floor and the body can sway gently. The travelling step is danced the same way, as is dancing in a circle round and back.

Doubles

When there are more than four couples, two standing couples (top or bottom) may dance 'doubles'. For example, when 'The Duke of Perth' (see p. 106) is danced in a five-couple set, the progressions are as follows:

1. The 1st couple dance with the 2nd and 3rd couples (4th and 5th stand).
2. Second time through, original 2nd couple stand at the top while 1st, 3rd and 4th couples dance and 5th couple stand.
3. Third time through, original 2nd and 3rd couples stand at the top while 1st, 4th and 5th couples dance. Instead of standing, the top two couples (old 2nd and 3rd) can dance doubles:-
   (a) 1st couple turn with the right hand, cast off one place, turn with the left hand to finish back-to-back between the 2nd couple, facing the opposite side.
   (b) For 'corner, partner, corner, partner', turn the person you are facing with the right hand, your partner with the left hand, and the same person with the right hand again.
   (c) For 'set and turn corners', set and turn the person you are facing twice.
   (d) For 'reels of three on the side', dance a reel of four across the dance, starting by giving right shoulder to the person you are facing. Finish with the 1st couple back in *top* place ready to start the dance normally with the 2nd and 3rd couples.

Equally, when the original 1st couple finish in fourth place after the third time through, they can dance doubles with the 5th couple. Dance exactly as above, except that at the end of the reel of four, the 1st couple must finish at the *bottom* (fifth place) and the 5th couple in fourth place.

It is also possible to dance some other dances as doubles simply by adapting them in the same way; however, the 'Duke of Perth' is the most usual.

Turning

For a one-handed turn, the forearm or elbow grip is the best way, providing it is done correctly. Both partners must be close together, with upper arms vertical and forearms parallel to the floor. Each dancer's elbow is cupped in the palm of his or her partner's hand, ensuring that the thumb is underneath; if it isn't, then the upper arm can be bruised. Dancers should never link arms as it is dangerous: if one person should slip, there is no support from his or her partner, and if the man is in Highland dress, his silver cuff buttons could scratch or cut his partner's arm. Similarly, dancers are advised not to use the thumb grip, that is, hands pointing upwards and clasping each other's thumbs.

Spinning or birling

When spinning, dancers should take their partner's right arms in an elbow grip and clasp their left hands on top; it is then quite safe to spin at speed. If one dancer should slip, the other can provide support. It is essential that both dancers must turn together; the man should not pivot on the spot, swinging his partner round at top speed. Do not use crossed wrists or gripped thumbs when spinning as this offers no mutual support, and accidents can, and do, happen. Dance with controlled abandon!

'The Reel of the 51st Division', Aberdonian style

In some areas, 'The Reel of the 51st Division'(see p.159) is danced all the way down the line, with every other couple starting. The top man or a steward will count 1-2, 1-2, etc.

1. All the 1st couples start; set, cast off (but as there is only one place to go, come in towards each other first) and lead up to face first corners.
2. Everyone in the line will be a first corner except the top woman's and the bottom man's position. Set to first corner, turn with the right hand, and keeping hold of corner's hand join left hand with partner and all set in diagonal lines, 1st couple turning by the left hand to face second corners.
3. Everyone will be a second corner except top man's and bottom woman's position. 1st couple set to second corner, turn with the right hand, and all set in line again;1st couple turning to their own side.
4. For the last eight bars, the whole line takes hands to circle round and back. In this way, everyone dances all the time.

After set and turn corners, the correct way is to take hands in a line and all set, as explained above. However, the habit has crept in of the 1st couple grasping each other's hands as soon as they have turned their corners and spinning by the right for four bars, leaving out the setting. This spoils the appearance of the dance, which represents St Andrew's Cross (first corners are one 'arm' and second corners are the other 'arm'), and was devised under arduous conditions to represent the cap badge of the regiment.

'Petronella'

In some areas, 'Petronella' (see p.157) is danced with the 2nd couple joining in for all the dance, not just for the poussette.
1. The 2nd couple step up immediately while the 1st couple petronella turn.
2. The 2nd couple then set with the 1st couple and continue to petronella turn and set, following the 1st couple (as in 'The Lea Rig' [see p.143]), until bars 15–16, when the 2nd couple, instead of setting, dance to place. If the 2nd couple insist on following the 1st couple down the middle and back, they must finish in second place, so the 1st couple come back under an arch made by the 2nd couple.

'Inverness Country Dance'

In a variation of the 'Inverness Country Dance' (see p.133), when the 1st couple lead down the middle and back, they must finish in second place, facing first corners; if the 2nd couple follow, they must lead back to top place. Another variation has the 2nd couple leading down followed by the 1st couple, and the 2nd couple must go back up under an arch made by 1st couple.

Advance and retire (see p.48)

An alternative form, in reel and jig time, is:
1. 2 walking steps forward (right-left): 3 stamps on the spot (right-left-right).
2. 2 walking steps backward (left-right); 3 claps (no movement).

Index

Dances are identified in the following index by **bold** type. The information given in parenthesis after each dance title is a reference to the catalogue number of recordings of music appropriate for that particular dance; those prefixed by 'A-' indicate that a recording is available from The Royal Scottish Country Dance Society, 12 Coates Crescent, Edinburgh EH3 7AH (tel. 0131-225 3854) while 'B-' indicates that a recording is available from The Scottish National Dance Company, 1 Lakeside, Earley, Reading RG6 7PG (tel. 01734-666006).